We cannot grow spiritually as we ought to in isolation from one another. We need to be supporting each other in love and prayer. One way to demonstrate our concern is by

Encouraging One Another

Welcome to a challenging study on the theme of encouragement—one of the keys to effective body function in the church.

Encouraging One Another

Gene A. Getz

While this book is designed for the reader's personal enjoyment and profit, it is also intended for group study. A leader's guide is available from your local Christian bookstore or from the publisher.

VICTOR
BOOKS a division of SP Publications, Inc.
WHEATON. ILLINOIS 60187

Offices also in
Whitby, Ontario, Canada
Amersham-on-the-Hill, Bucks, England

Third printing, 1983

Most of the Scripture quotations in this book are from the *New International Version,* © 1978 by The New York International Bible Society. Other quotations are from the King James Version (KJV) and the *New American Standard Bible* (NASB), © 1960, 1962, 1963, 1968, 1971, 1972, 1973 by the Lockman Foundation, La Habra, California. Used by permission.

Recommended Dewey Decimal Classification: 248.4
  Suggested Subject Headings: Christian Life; Spiritual Life

Library of Congress Catalog Card Number: 80-54724
ISBN: 0-88207-256-0

VICTOR BOOKS
A division of SP Publications, Inc.
P.O. Box 1825 ● Wheaton, Illinois 60187

CONTENTS

ACKNOWLEDGEMENT

I wish to thank my good friend, John Best, a professor in the Department of New Testament Literature and Exegesis at Dallas Theological Seminary and a participating member of the body of Christ at Fellowship Bible Church. John both heard me deliver this series of messages and also read the manuscript before it was published and offered some very helpful suggestions.

Thanks also to his wife, Carolyn, who has on various occasions exemplified principles in this book by creatively sharing some very meaningful thoughts and experiences in our weekly sharing service.

LOOKING AHEAD

No personal study in the New Testament has impacted my own life more than this one on mutual encouragement. And no series of messages has brought more positive feedback. Both biblically and pragmatically I've discovered that there is a great need for Christians to encourage one another.

This study begins with an exhortation to the body of Christ to meet together regularly to carry out this process. As we continue in our biblical study, we quickly discover it is possible to carry out the "encouraging" exhortations primarily because of the Holy Spirit, whom Jesus called the Great Encourager.

A major part of this study follows the chronological and sequential development of Christianity in the Book of Acts. Very early in the history of the church, Barnabas walks on stage and takes the lead role as an encourager. In fact, his name actually means "son of encouragement."

Eventually, a second person, Saul of Tarsus, joins Barnabas in modeling the process of encouragement. There's no more exciting study in Scripture than to see and experience how Barnabas impacted this man's life. Though at one point these men separated because of a sharp disagreement, the influence of Barnabas' encouragement lifestyle on Paul stands out boldly on the pages of Scripture. It is particularly reflected in Paul's letters to the churches.

Welcome then to a challenging study on the theme of encouragement. It is one of the keys to effective body function in the church. Though there are many things we are to do to build each other up as Christians, no function is more important than mutual encouragement.

Gene A. Getz

1

Meeting Together

I remember hearing a friend of mine speak on one occasion. He made a specific effort to show a group of Christians that—as individual believers—they did not need other Christians in their lives in order to grow spiritually. Following his presentation, he opened the meeting for questions and comments.

At that juncture I felt deeply constrained to point out that he had overlooked an important fact. Great portions of the New Testament clearly emphasize that Christians *do* need one another in order to grow spiritually. My friend was concerned that some Christians he knew had developed an overdependence on other Christians rather than on Jesus Christ—which is indeed possible. But he had fallen prey to the peril of the pendulum. He had overreacted to an overreaction.

Our relationship to Christ in salvation is a personal experience. We must *individually* receive Christ as Saviour and Lord. And we must continue to nurture that relationship through *personal* communication and worship. But unless we are a vital part of the functioning body of Christ, we will not grow into well-balanced Christians. We need the ministry of others in our lives in order to become mature in Jesus Christ.

Many words used by New Testament writers describe the functioning body of Christ and what believers are to do for one another. But no word is used more frequently than the basic Greek word *parakaleō*. This word is often translated, particularly in our more recent versions, "to encourage."

9

The most comprehensive New Testament passage instructing us to *encourage one another* appears in the letter to the Hebrews. We do not know for sure who wrote this letter, but many believe it was Paul. Some believe it was Apollos. But there is a good possibility it may have been Barnabas, and as we study this man's ministry style, we'll see why.

The passage is found in Hebrews 10, verses 19-26. The specific injunction reads, "Let us not give up *meeting together,* as some are in the habit of doing, but let us *encourage one another*—and all the more as you see the Day approaching" (v. 25).[1]

Though the specific words *one another* are not used in the original text of verse 25, they are used in verse 24. The idea in verse 25 is an extension of this concept. Therefore, the translators are very much in order to use the words *one another* in verse 25.

This passage helps us understand what it means to "encourage one another." It includes the *setting,* the *goals,* and the primary *means* for this mutual process.

"Encouraging One Another"—The Setting

The author of this letter states: "Let us not give up *meeting together.*" Though true Christianity uniquely involves a *personal* relationship with Jesus Christ, it is also a *corporate* experience. This passage underscores that fact. Christians cannot grow spiritually as they ought to in isolation from one another.

This passage introduces us to the ever-prevalent theme of the New Testament—the importance of the functioning body of Christ. As Paul stated in his letter to the Ephesians, for the body of Christ to grow and build itself up in love, each part *must* do its work. "The whole body," Paul wrote, is "joined and held together by *every supporting ligament*" (Eph. 4:16). In the Book of Hebrews we learn that one aspect of this building work is mutual encouragement.

This is the *setting.* We are not to "give up meeting together, *as some are in the habit of doing,* but let us encourage one another—and all the more as you see the Day approaching" (Heb. 10:25). In the first-century church, Christians were beginning to neglect meeting together. No doubt they were even losing sight of

---

[1]Hereafter, all italicized words in Scripture references are used for emphasis.

the fact that Jesus Christ could come at any moment to take them home to heaven. Neglecting to meet together caused them to fail to "encourage one another" regularly so that they would be prepared to meet Christ at His return. Belief in the Lord's imminent return became an important motivational factor in furthering the corporate life of the New Testament church.

"Encouraging One Another"—The Goals

What should happen to Christians when they meet together regularly and "encourage one another"? The goals for this process are clearly outlined in this passage from Hebrews.

Ordinarily it is best to explain a Scripture passage chronologically and sequentially. However, to get the full impact of this section of Scripture, it helps to begin with what we might call the "bottom line"—"meeting together to encourage one another." Then we'll move back through the passage to see *why* Christians should meet together (refer to the diagram of this passage).

1. We should grow in our faith (Heb. 10:22). Christians should meet together for mutual encouragement so that we might grow in our *faith.* Thus we read, "Let us draw near to God with a sincere heart in *full assurance of faith*" (10:22).

Faith is an essential ingredient in our relationship with God. "Without *faith* it is impossible to please God, because anyone who comes to Him must *believe* that He exists and that He rewards those who earnestly seek Him" (11:6).

But what is faith? "Now faith is being *sure* of what we hope for and *certain* of what we do not see" (v. 1). *What we hope for* involves the promises God has given us in His Word. *What we do not see* involves the reality of God Himself and of His Son, Jesus Christ. Jesus was indeed a Man of history. But He now sits at God's right hand—making it possible for us to enter into God's holy presence through prayer and worship.

Every Christian has direct access to God. We need no priest, minister, or intercessor except Jesus Christ Himself. We can draw near to Him with "full assurance of faith" because of what Christ has done in our hearts. We've been cleansed from our sins by His blood. We no longer have to be in bondage to guilt.

A growing and deepening faith reflects that God is not

The Means

19 Therefore, brothers,
   since we have confidence to enter the most holy place
20   by the blood of Jesus,
       by a new and loving way
           opened for us through the curtain,
                       that is, His body,

21 And
   since we have a great priest over the house of God,

The Goals

22 Let us draw near to God
       with a sincere heart
       in *full assurance of FAITH*,
   having our hearts sprinkled to cleanse us from a guilty conscience
       and
       having our bodies washed with pure water.

23 Let us hold unswervingly to the *HOPE we profess*,
   for He who promised is faithful.

24 And let us consider how we may *spur one another on*
                       toward LOVE
                           and
                           good deeds.

The Setting

25 Let us not give up meeting together, as some are in the habit of doing,
       but
   let us *encourage one another*—and all the more as you see the day approaching.
                                           Hebrews 10:19-25

merely an academic idea. Though He is an invisible Spirit, He is a real personality to whom we can communicate and relate with feeling and warmth. He is indeed the God who is there, and His Son, Jesus Christ, sits at His right hand allowing us into His very presence. When we gather together regularly, we are to "encourage one another" to approach God in this way—to trust Him for every detail of our lives. As we do, we'll grow together in faith.

In my own church I have been deeply impressed and greatly encouraged by other Christians who have approached God with sincere faith. Through their prayers and responses, I have sensed that God is very real to them. I've seen God honor their faith and this has *encouraged me* to develop my own trust relationship with God even more.

2. We should grow in our hope (Heb. 10:23). Our faith is one area that is affected by mutual encouragement. So is our *hope.* Consequently we read, "Let us hold unswervingly to the *hope* we profess" (10:23).

Hope, though it is a distinctive quality, is always clearly aligned with faith. Hope focuses more on *what* Christians believe than on *whom* we believe in. Obviously it is impossible to have one without the other. However, it *is* possible to be strong in faith and weak in hope.

This is clearly illustrated in the lives of the Thessalonican Christians. When Paul wrote his first letter to them, he thanked God for their "work produced by *faith,*" their "labor prompted by *love,*" and their "endurance inspired by *hope*" (1 Thes. 1:3). But in his second letter, his emphasis was different. "We ought always to thank God for you, brothers, and rightly so," Paul wrote, "because your *faith is growing more and more,* and the love every one of you has for each other *is increasing*" (2 Thes. 1:3). However, Paul said nothing about their *hope.*

Why not? The answer is clear when we understand that sometime between the first and second letter, someone had "unsettled" or "alarmed" them. They had heard "that the day of the Lord had already come" (2:2). Obviously this disturbed their "endurance inspired by hope." No longer did they believe they would be delivered from the great judgments that were coming upon the earth. They mistakenly believed that judgment had already come.

Paul immediately corrected this false impression. "Stand firm," he wrote, "and hold to the *teachings* we passed on to you" (v. 15). Then Paul said something that relates specifically to what we read in the Hebrew letter: "May our Lord Jesus Christ Himself and God our Father, who loved us and by His grace gave us *eternal encouragement* and good *hope, encourage* your hearts and strengthen you in every good deed and word" (vv. 16-17). At this point Paul is *encouraging* these believers with correct doctrine. Though they had a growing and developing faith in God, they were uninformed doctrinally, which disturbed their hope.

Another goal, then, of mutual Christian encouragement is to help us "hold unswervingly to the *hope we profess,* for He who promised is faithful" (Heb. 10:23). The Thessalonicans were confused in one major doctrinal area, which affected their hope of deliverance from earthly judgments. There are, however, other doctrinal areas that can also affect our hope.

For example, I grew up in a church where I was not taught to really *know* that I had eternal life. I was always uncertain of my spiritual condition before God. I lacked *hope* of eternal life, though I was trusting Christ the best I knew how.

One day, while studying the Bible as a student at Moody Bible Institute, I realized I could know for *sure* that I was saved. I remember that moment as if it were yesterday. Suddenly I saw clearly that it really didn't matter how I *felt* about my relationship with God. My eternal destiny was based, not on my feelings, but on what God says. The Apostle John's words became real to me: "Whoever believes in the Son *has* eternal life" (John 3:36). Once I understood this great doctrinal truth, I had a steadfast hope. No longer did I wonder if I was a Christian one day and not the next. I became convinced that nothing would be able to separate me "from the love of God that is in Christ Jesus our Lord" (Rom. 8:39). I had *hope!*

3. *We should grow in our love (Heb. 10:24).* More than any other quality, mutual encouragement among members of the body of Christ should "spur one another on toward *love* and good deeds" (v. 24). Paul underscored this truth when writing to the Corinthians. Summarizing at the end of that great passage in 1 Corinthians he said, "And now these three re-

main: faith, hope, and love. But the greatest of these is *love*" (1 Cor. 13:13).

Love, however, is not automatic. If it were, the author of the letter to the Hebrews would not have exhorted the Hebrew Christians to "consider *how*" to "spur one another on toward love and good deeds." Neither would Paul have admonished the Corinthians to "follow the way of love" (1 Cor. 14:1). Peter would not have told us to "love each other deeply" (1 Peter 4:8). The Apostle John would not have again and again in his first epistle emphasized, "Love one another." Love must be nurtured and developed among Christians. We must give careful thought as to *how* we can motivate each other to practice this important Christian virtue.

"Encouraging One Another"—The Means

At this point we've looked at the *setting* for encouraging one another—we must meet together regularly. Secondly, we have looked at the *goals* of this process—to develop our *faith*, our *hope, and our love*. Thirdly, let's look at the primary *means* for mutual encouragement—God's truth as revealed in His Son, Jesus Christ, and in His written Word, the Bible. This is the essence of what we read in Hebrews 10:19-22: "Therefore, brothers, since we have confidence to enter the Most Holy Place by the blood of Jesus, by a new and living way opened for us through the curtain, that is, His body, and since we have a great Priest over the house of God, let us draw near to God."

With this brief *therefore* statement the author summarized both Jewish and Christian history. In the Old Testament, God established a covenant with His people based on a sacrificial system administered by human priests. He instructed them to build a tabernacle (see diagram). In the outer court stood the *brass altar* where animals were sacrificed to God. The *laver* stood about midway between the altar and the tabernacle itself and served as a basin priests used for ceremonial washings. In the first part of the tabernacle—called the Holy Place—stood the *table of showbread,* the *golden candlestick,* and the *altar of incense.* In the Most Holy Place, separated from the Holy Place by a *veil,* stood the *Ark of*

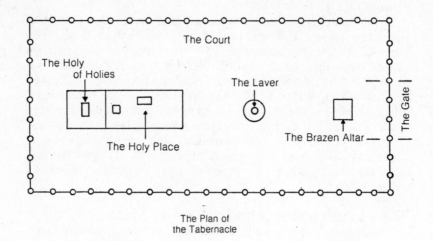

The Plan of
the Tabernacle

the Covenant. The lid of the ark was called the *Mercy Seat.* It was here in the Holy of Holies that God's presence dwelt in a very special way. Later a temple was built to replace the tabernacle. The temple was very similar in structure, but much more elaborate.

The high priest alone could enter the Most Holy Place, and only once a year and after proper ceremonial preparation. To violate these ceremonial laws would bring sudden death—even to the high priest.

When Jesus Christ came into this world He established a new covenant based on His death and resurrection. He became the perfect sacrifice for sin. When He died, the veil in the temple was supernaturally torn from the top to the bottom, indicating that nothing stands between God and any man who has placed his faith in Jesus Christ for forgiveness of sins. We can enter into the "Most Holy Place"—God's presence—anytime and anywhere. We need no earthly intercessor or priest. Jesus Christ Himself *is* our great *High Priest.* Through His shed blood and torn body, symbolized by the rent veil, we can enter into God's presence without fear of rejection or death. As Paul stated in his first letter to Timothy, "There is *one God* and *one Mediator* between God and man, the Man Christ Jesus, who gave Himself as a ransom for all men" (1 Tim. 2:5-6).

This then is the message in Hebrews 10:19-24:

> Therefore, brothers, since we have confidence to enter the Most Holy Place by the blood of Jesus, by a new and living way opened for us through the curtain, that is, His body, and since we have a great Priest over the house of God, let us draw near to God with a sincere heart in full assurance of faith. . . . Let us hold unswervingly to the hope we profess. . . . And let us consider how we may spur one another on toward love and good deeds.

This is indeed *good news!* "In the past God spoke to our forefathers through the prophets at many times and in various ways, but in these last days He has spoken to us by His Son, whom He appointed heir of all things, and through whom He made the universe" (1:1-2).

In summary, this is the message of the Bible. Page after page unfolds for us this great redemptive story. It began in the Book of Exodus with the Law of Moses and ends with the first coming of Jesus Christ who fulfilled all of the demands of the Law and became the reality that was foreshadowed in the tabernacle. The *cross* replaced the *brass altar.* Christ's ability to *cleanse us* from all sin replaced the *laver.* As the *Light* of the world and the *Bread* of life, Christ replaced the *golden candlestick* and the *table of showbread.* As our constant *Intercessor,* He replaced the *altar of incense.* And with His *rent body* which was torn by the nails and the spear, He removed the *veil* that separated sinful mankind from God's holy presence. The sacrifice of Himself was "once for all" (7:27). Once He offered Himself He then "sat down at the right hand of the throne of the Majesty in heaven" (8:1).

Without the message of the Scriptures we would have nothing with which to encourage one another. We would have no purpose for meeting together. Our knowledge of God would be so limited we would have no rational object for our faith, no doctrine on which to build our hope, and no way of even knowing the meaning of genuine love. As John stated, "This is how we know what love is: Jesus Christ laid down His life for us. And we ought to lay down our lives for our brothers" (1 John 3:16).

A 20th-Century Perspective and Life Response

The primary concern of the author of the Hebrew letter was that we *meet together regularly* in order to encourage one another with these great biblical truths, and to practice them in our lives—reflecting a growing faith, hope, and love. But Christians today are thwarted in carrying out this biblical injunction for at least four reasons.

1. Many competing activities in our culture make it easy for Christians to neglect meeting together regularly. All believers should establish biblical priorities. One of those priorities should be to meet regularly with other Christians. This is not a legislative rule, but a basic biblical injunction—one which we have seen quite clearly focused in the letter to the Hebrews.

Unfortunately, some Christians get sidetracked from meeting together by becoming involved exclusively in what some have called the "electric church." That is, their regular "church attendance" involves watching Christian programs on television or listening to them on the radio. Rather than using this 20th-century blessing as a supplement to their fellowship in a local church, thousands of Christians substitute this kind of religious programming for live, flesh-and-blood experiences with other Christians. Unfortunately, there is no adequate substitute for face-to-face Christian fellowship.

2. Most churches' weekly services are designed for Christians to "meet together regularly" but not to provide opportunities for body function and mutual encouragement. In many churches, congregational meetings give members no more opportunity for involvement in one another's lives than sitting in front of a television set. People by and large are spectators in both settings. Unfortunately, this kind of "church life" does not measure up to God's plan. Our churches' services should be designed to foster and promote body function.

3. Many Christians do not live as though Christ may return at any moment. It is clear that the author of the letter to the Hebrews used this great doctrinal truth as a means to motivate Christians in the first century to "meet together regularly" and to

What other activities, both religious and secular,
interfere with your involvement in the lives of other Christians?

RELIGIOUS ACTIVITIES	SECULAR ACTIVITIES
_____	_____
_____	_____
_____	_____
_____	_____
_____	_____
_____	_____
_____	_____
_____	_____

"encourage one another." If this was necessary in the 1st-century world, how much more so is it needed in the 20th-century world?

To what extent does your belief that Christ could return at any moment affect your involvement in other Christians' lives? The following multiple choice statement may help you answer this question:

I think about Christ's second coming . . .

__ Never; __ A little; __ Some; __ Frequently.

4. *Many Christians do not know the Bible well enough to use it naturally and as a regular means to encourage other Christians.* Obviously, this is one reason why Christians should gather together regularly—to have vital learning experiences with the Word of God. Today, however, we have access to many versions of the Bible which allow us to study it on our own. This of course should not be a substitute for group Bible study. Individual study of the Scriptures is a great privilege—one that is relatively new in the history of the world. We can take advantage of this opportunity to learn more of God's truths in order to take part more effectively when members of the body of Christ meet for mutual encouragement.

How do the structures in your church encourage or discourage
other believers to be involved in one another's lives/

WAYS IN WHICH
OUR CHURCH STRUCTURES:

Encourage
Body Function:

Discourage
Body Function:

_____   _____

_____   _____

_____   _____

_____   _____

_____   _____

_____   _____

_____   _____

_____   _____

_____   _____

To what extent are you studying the Bible regularly, both in
groups as well as individually? Complete the following sentence:
"I realize that I am not studying the Bible as regularly as I should.
Therefore, I will . . .

_____

_____

_____."

2

The Great Encourager

Why is it possible for Christians to meet together for mutual encouragement? It's because we have something with which to encourage one another.

But to answer this question more adequately, we must go back to an important conversation Jesus Christ had with the apostles shortly before His death. They gathered together in the Upper Room where they shared in the Passover meal. Several things happened that evening that deeply disturbed and troubled them.

First, Christ had insisted on washing their feet—a humbling experience for all of them, particularly since they had been arguing among themselves about who was going to be the greatest in God's kingdom (John 13:1-17).

Second, Christ had singled out Judas as His betrayer—an event that not only threatened the other 11 apostles, but troubled Jesus Christ Himself. We read that He "was *troubled* in spirit and testified, 'I tell you the truth, one of you is going to betray Me'" (v. 21).

Third, Jesus told His men He was going to leave them—a statement that left them bewildered. "I will be with you only a little longer," He said. "You will look for Me, and just as I told the Jews, so I tell you now: Where I am going you cannot come" (v. 33).

Peter was first to respond. "Lord, where are You going?" (v. 36)

But Jesus' answer only added to their insecurity. "Where I

am going, you cannot follow now, but you will follow later"
(v. 36)

Jesus, knowing their feelings of uncertainty, spoke directly to
their confused thoughts and emotions: "Do not let your hearts be
troubled," He reassured them. "Trust in God; trust also in Me. In
My Father's house are many rooms; if it were not so, I would have
told you. I am going there to prepare a place for you. And if I go
and prepare a place for you, I will come back and take you to be
with Me that you also may be where I am" (14:1-3).

These were strange words to the apostles. In no way could they
relate to what Jesus was saying. They were confused and frustrated
even more when Jesus said, "You know the way to the place where
I am going" (v. 4).

Though Thomas reflected his own frustration and anxiety, he no
doubt represented *all* the men when he blurted out, "Lord, we
don't know *where* You are going, so *how* can we know the *way?*"
(v. 5)

From an earthly point of view, this was a logical question. But
Jesus was not speaking geographically. He was talking about
eternal and spiritual issues that centered in Himself and in His
purpose for coming into the world. His answer was startling and
profound: "I am the *way* and the *truth* and the *life.* No one comes
to the Father except through Me" (v. 6).

If Thomas was impatient—and he no doubt was—Philip tried to
be teachable. "Lord," he said, *"show us* the Father and that will
be enough for us" (v. 8).

Jesus' pedagogical plan was right on schedule. The confusion He
had created was by design—that the apostles might sense a deep
need and listen and learn. With that key question from Philip,
Jesus zeroed in on the essence of Christianity—the reason it is
unique and distinct from all of the world's religions. Though the
apostles' questions reflected spiritual ignorance, these men were
indeed asking the *right* questions—questions Jesus wanted them to
ask. "Don't you know Me, Philip, even after I have been among
you such a long time? Anyone who has seen Me has seen the
Father" (v. 9).

Though they would not yet grasp its total meaning, the apostles
were ready to hear about the next major truth from the lips of
Jesus—one so profound that, for nearly 2,000 years, it has made it

possible for people everywhere to experience the dynamic power of Christianity. As we shall see, it was this part of God's plan and promise that *has* (1) *preserved* for us through the centuries what Jesus taught while on earth; that *has* (2) *interpreted* more clearly what He taught; that *has* (3) *given* mankind additional truth to enable us to understand God's eternal plan for all mankind; and *has* (4) *guaranteed* His presence with each of His children forever.

What was this plan? "I will ask the Father," Jesus said, "and He will give you another Counselor to be with you forever—the Spirit of Truth" (vv. 16-17).

"Another Counselor"

Following Christ's return to heaven, God's plan for continuing what His Son had begun focused on the Holy Spirit. Four times in this passage Jesus identified the Holy Spirit as a *"Counselor"* (vv. 16, 26; 15:26; 16:7). Translators of the *King James Version* call Him "another *Comforter*." In the *New American Standard Bible* He is identified as "another *Helper*."

Why these different English titles? The word in the language of the Greek New Testament is *paraklētos,* transliterated into English as "another *paraclete*." The important correlation here is that the Greek verb, *parakaleō* is frequently translated "to encourage." Therefore, it would seem appropriate to identify the Holy Spirit in this passage as "another Encourager," especially in view of the context in which John refers to the coming of the Holy Spirit and what He will do.

Kenneth Wuest, in his *Word Studies in the Greek New Testament,* reminds us that the word *paraclete* "was used in the first century of one called in to support another or give him aid. It was a technical term to describe a lawyer in the Greek law courts, one who was called in to aid the accused." But referring to Jesus' use of the word Wuest states, "We do not have to deal with the law, for a Christian is not under law, but under grace. Therefore, the word here merely means 'one called in to help another'" (Eerdman's, p. 90).

At this time in their lives, the apostles were very fearful. Their hearts were "troubled" (John 14:27). Hatred toward them from the religious leaders had never been more intense. It was no secret that there had been several attempts to kill their leader. This was why Jesus "no longer moved about publicly" (11:54). No wonder these men were frightened and discouraged when Jesus announced His plans to leave them!

In actuality Jesus was not going to leave them. He would still be with them in the person of the Holy Spirit. This was why He said, "The world cannot accept Him [this Counselor] because it neither sees Him nor knows Him. But *you know Him, for He lives with you and will be in you*" (14:17). With this statement Jesus introduced them to the Holy Spirit. Though the Spirit is a separate Person in the Godhead, yet He is one with the Father and the Son. He who had seen the Son had seen the Father; likewise, he who had seen the Son had also seen the Holy Spirit. They are three Persons, yet one God. And Jesus while on earth, revealed them all.

The Holy Spirit was then to be "another Counselor"—another *Encourager*. He would continue Christ's work on earth. He would never leave the apostles—or others who followed Christ. But *how* would He counsel them, comfort them, and encourage them? Jesus made that point very clear.

"The Spirit of Truth"

Three times in this setting Jesus referred to the One who was coming as the Spirit of Truth (14:17; 15:26; 16:13). Furthermore, Jesus described the Holy Spirit's primary function.

- But the Counselor, the Holy Spirit, whom the Father will send in My name, will *teach* you *all things* and will *remind you* of *everything I have said to you* (14:26).

- When the Counselor comes, whom I will send to you from the Father, the Spirit of Truth who goes out from the Father, *He will testify about Me* (15:26).

- Unless I go away, the Counselor will not come to you; but if I go, I will send Him to you. When He comes, He will convict the world of guilt in regard to *sin* and *righteousness* and *judgment* (16:7-8).

- I have much more to say to you, more than you can now bear. But when He, the Spirit of Truth, comes, He will *guide* you into *all truth*. He will not speak on His own; He will speak only what He hears, and He will *tell* you *what is yet to come* (vv 12-13).

One of the primary reasons the Holy Spirit came to earth was to continue Jesus' teaching ministry. In the apostles' time, the Holy Spirit used four ways to fulfill His task.

First, He helped them recall what Jesus had taught during the last years of His life. Much of what Jesus had said they did not understand or had forgotten.

Second, the Spirit testified that Jesus Christ was indeed the Son of God and the Saviour of the world. When the Holy Spirit came this is exactly what happened, for we read, "God also testified to it [this salvation] by signs, wonders, and various miracles, and gifts of the Holy Spirit distributed according to His will" (Heb. 2:4).

Third, the Holy Spirit clearly spelled out God's will regarding right and wrong and how God had provided for man's salvation.

Fourth, the Holy Spirit completed God's revelation, clearly revealing God's future plan for all mankind. Thus, Jesus said, "He will tell you *what is yet to come.*"

"Encouraged by the Holy Spirit"

Though the 11 apostles did not yet understand all of Jesus' statements about the Holy Spirit, they were soon to find out. Following Christ's death, resurrection, and ascension they and a small band of believers waited in Jerusalem as Jesus had told them to (Luke 24:49). And while there, the Holy Spirit came as Jesus had promised. It was a dramatic event. He *gifted* some of them so they would be able to recall, understand, and communicate God's truth. He *empowered* some of them to work miracles in order to verify the message they were teaching.

And most important for us living today, He *inspired* some to write down God's message—God's Truth—in permanent form. The Gospels tell us what Jesus said and did during His earthly ministry; the Book of Acts reveals the coming of the Holy Spirit, the founding of the church, and the spread of Christianity. The epistles instruct us in sound doctrine—*what* to believe and *how* to live in the light of God's mercy and grace. The Book of Revelation reveals "what is yet to come" (John 16:13; Rev. 1:19).

Relative to Christ's specific promise that He would send

"another Counselor" or "Encourager," there's a significant verse recorded in the Book of Acts. Following Saul's conversion to Christianity, persecution ceased throughout the New Testament world. We read:

> Then the church throughout Judea, Galilee, and Samaria enjoyed a time of peace. It was *strengthened;* and *encouraged by the Holy Spirit;* it grew in numbers, living in the fear of the Lord (Acts 9:31).

Here indeed is a direct reference to what Jesus said would happen when the Holy Spirit came. As promised, He would strengthen and encourage them. How? By revealing truth. By teaching them and guiding them as Jesus had said He would.

How did this take place? Another passage in Acts lets us see the human side of this process. After Paul and Barnabas founded churches in Lystra, Iconium, and Antioch, we read that they returned to these cities *"strengthening* the disciples and *encouraging* them to remain true to the faith"* (Acts 14:22).

Obviously, the means of encouragement was God's message of truth revealed to these apostles directly by the Holy Spirit. Here again we see a specific fulfillment of what Jesus had promised His apostles in the Upper Room.

The Holy Spirit and 20th-Century Christians

The direct application of what we have studied in John's Gospel is clear. One of God's primary means of encouraging Christians everywhere is with truth—truth revealed by the Holy Spirit. The repository of that truth is the Bible. That is why Paul wrote, "For everything that was *written* in the past was written to teach us, so that through endurance and the *encouragement of the Scriptures* we might have hope" (Rom. 15:4).

And to Timothy he wrote, "All Scripture is *God-breathed* [inspired by the Holy Spirit] and is useful for teaching, rebuking, correcting, and training in righteousness, so that the man of God may be thoroughly equipped for every good work" (2 Tim. 3:16-17).

The Apostle Peter also referred to the ministry of the Holy Spirit in revealing God's will. "Above all," he wrote in his second epistle, "You must understand that no *prophecy of Scripture* came about by the prophet's own interpretation. For prophecy never had its origin in the will of man, but men spoke from God as they were carried along by the Holy Spirit" (2 Peter 1:20-21).

Though Peter is referring to Old Testament prophets, his statement also applies to what Jesus promised His 11 men in the Upper Room. Many of them were inspired by the Holy Spirit to record God's Word in Holy Writ—which we call the New Testament. When He came upon them He was indeed "another Encourager" and the "Spirit of Truth." Though Jesus was Himself "the Truth," the Holy Spirit has continued to this day to reveal through the Scriptures all that Jesus meant when He told the apostles, "I am the way and the truth and the life. No one comes to the Father except through Me" (John 14:6).

Two Extremes
When approaching the subject of the Holy Spirit, some Christians go to one of two extremes.

1. An academic approach to the Christian life. In New Testament times, the Holy Spirit revealed Truth to certain Christians and inspired them to record that truth for us in the New Testament. As a result, some groups strongly emphasize studying, understanding, and obeying Scripture and neglect the part the Holy Spirit *as a Person* plays in our lives. This leads to what we might call an academic or intellectual Christian experience. The Holy Spirit is either regarded as totally "passive," or an "idea," or an "influence."

I was talking to a man one day whose brother was a minister in a Christian denomination. The man and his brother had gotten into a discussion regarding the work of the Holy Spirit. "Oh," the minister stated, "the Word of God and the Holy Spirit are the same."

Obviously, this viewpoint would lead to a very intellectual approach to Christianity. This is of course an extreme view. And one reason some people hold this view is because of other Christians who have gone to the opposite extreme.

2. An experiential approach to the Christian life. Other Christians do not understand the unique role the Holy Spirit played in the early days of Christianity. They try to duplicate in their own lives—and sincerely so—everything that Jesus taught (for example, John 14—16). They do not understand the concepts of divine revelation and inspiration. They fail to realize that in the early days of Christianity, the Holy Spirit spoke *directly* to some Christians (particularly the apostles) which enabled them to record God's truths. These Christians' belief that the Holy Spirit is continuing that process even today, often causes them to interpret various mental impressions, ideas, and feelings as coming directly from the Holy Spirit. This kind of mystical theology has led to all kinds of extreme behaviors within Christianity. In many instances it has led to the establishing of various cults and "isms" that depart from the direct teachings of the Bible.

Let me illustrate what I mean. One Sunday afternoon a total stranger telephoned me. He promptly informed me that "the Holy Spirit had given him my name" and wondered if I knew why the Holy Spirit would have done that.

I was taken back at first. But I then began to ask some questions. I found out that this man was planning to come to Dallas to start a new ministry—and *probably* wanted me to help him get started.

After a brief conversation, I was firmly convinced the Holy Spirit had not given this man my name. If he was sincere—and possibly he was—I believe that he was sincerely wrong. He had become a victim of a certain kind of experiential theology that does not harmonize with the Scriptures.

I remember the comment a minister made as he listened to some Christian music. "Oh," he said, "when I listen to that record, the Holy Spirit just makes my spine tingle."

Even as a rather uninformed Christian at that time, I knew something was wrong with his theology. Lots of experiences in life can make our "spines tingle"—even music that is *not* spiritual.

We can experience emotions from many sources. We can have mental impressions that come from our subconscious or from our conscious nature. Much of what we *think* often relates to what we *want*. Psychological and mental phenomena are often dangerous guidelines for living the Christian life. They can lead us into all kinds of wrong conclusions regarding the work of the Holy Spirit in our lives.

A Balanced Approach to the Christian Life

What does the Bible teach about the Holy Spirit? Obviously, it's impossible to answer this question completely in this brief chapter. However, let's consider significant points.

First, we must realize that the Holy Spirit was more actively and directly involved in certain Christians' lives in the New Testament world. Those believers had no New Testament literature. Their only means of learning God's truths was through certain gifted individuals who learned *directly* from God. However, once the Holy Spirit inspired men to record God's truths in the Bible, it is my personal conviction that direct revelation ceased. What Jesus promised for example in John 14—16 was basically fulfilled with the completed revelation of God as we have it in the New Testament.

This does not mean that God does not lead and direct His children today. However, *direct revelation* refers to specific verbal and sometimes visual communication from God. Today, this would certainly represent the exception and not the rule in God's communication with His children.

Second, we must realize this does not mean the Holy Spirit is not present in every Christian's life today. Though His specific roles and functions have changed, He wants to be continually active in our lives, particularly through the truth He has revealed in Scripture. His primary function today is to *illuminate* our hearts and minds so that we understand what He has revealed through those who wrote the Scriptures.

At this point we should remember that it's always very important to evaluate impressions, ideas, and experiences in the light of the revealed Word of God. If we do not, we could make some serious errors in judgment and behavior. I've known some Christians who have had certain "religious experiences" which contradicted the Bible. Yet they chose to follow their religious experiences rather than the Word of God. The results were spiritually disastrous.

Third, the Holy Spirit wants us to use what He has revealed in Scripture to *encourage one another.* As we've seen already from God's Word, this is the primary and basic means for "mutual encouragement." In the Bible we discover God's words, His plans for us, His promises, and His concerns. It is God's written Word that the Holy Spirit uses primarily to make our spiritual lives meaningful and to keep the body of Christ functioning according to God's will.

A Practical Illustration

Following is a scriptural survey of how the Holy Spirit uses the truth He has already revealed to teach, guide, and lead us. Without the revealed Word of God we would not know *how* to be saved from our sin, nor could we be *sure* of our salvation.

ASSURANCE OF SALVATION

The Spirit Himself testifies with our spirit that we are God's children (Rom. 8:16).

What has the Holy Spirit said to us that "testifies with our spirit that we are God's children"?

John 3:36	Whoever believes in the Son *has eternal life,* but whoever rejects the Son will not see life, for God's wrath remains on him.
John 5:24	I tell you the **truth,** whoever hears My word and believes Him who sent Me *has eternal life* and will not be condemned; he has crossed over from death to life.
Acts 16:31	Believe in the Lord Jesus, and *you will be saved*—you and your household.
Romans 6:23	For the wages of sin is death, but the gift of God *is eternal life* in Christ Jesus our Lord.
Romans 10:9	That if you confess with your mouth, "Jesus is Lord," and believe in your heart that God raised Him from the dead, *you will be saved.*

Ephesians 1:7-8   In Him we *have redemption* through His blood, the *forgiveness of sins,* in accordance with the riches of God's grace that He lavished on us with all wisdom and understanding.

1 John 5:11-13   And this is the testimony: God *has given us eternal life;* and this life is in His Son. He who has the Son *has life;* he who does not have the Son of God does not have life. I write these things to you who believe in the name of the Son of God so that you *may know* that you *have eternal life.*

What about you? Does the Holy Spirit bear witness with your spirit that you are God's child? He can—if you'll let Him. Believe the **truth** He has revealed and you can know for sure you're a Christian.

3

Barnabas—Son of Encouragement, Act I

As a young man, just 18 years old, I vividly remember leaving my Indiana farm home to go to Chicago and study at Moody Bible Institute. In those days 100 miles seemed like 1,000. Breaking away from a deeply ingrained religious tradition left me feeling confused—both theologically and emotionally. Even my parents were somewhat skeptical and unsupportive, for they knew the wrath of certain church officials would fall on them for allowing me to attend an evangelical Bible school.

For many months I was inwardly torn between what I was learning at MBI and what I had been previously taught. One professor sensed my confusion and distress. He spent many hours just listening to my life story, my beliefs, my questionings, and my doubts. In a non-judgmental way, he helped me clarify what I believed.

In the process he began to concentrate his comments on what he perceived as my personality strengths. Well aware of my doctrinal confusion, my emotional instability, and my spiritual immaturity, this professor kept focusing on my positive qualities. He was one of the first Christians who put his total confidence in me. Little by little I began to emerge from my theological and psychological quagmire. I began to be what he believed I could become.

That professor's name was Harold Garner. But he could have been called "Barnabas, Son of Encouragement"—for that is what he was to me. God used him to shape the direction of my life.

Humanly speaking, I would not have made it through the first semester at Moody Bible Institute without Dr. Garner's personal encouragement.

When it comes to mutual encouragement, Barnabas is definitely the biblical character the Holy Spirit wants us to pay particular attention to. Not only does the meaning of his name point to his lifestyle, but his attitudes and actions as recorded in Scripture demonstrate why the apostles named him "Barnabas, Son of Encouragement."

Barnabas serves as a unique Christian model for all believers. Let's pull back the curtain on the stage of divine history and look at *Barnabas—Son of Encouragement, Act I.*

The Historical Setting—Jerusalem, A.D. 33

As Jesus met together with His 11 men in the Upper Room, He sensed that they were theologically and psychologically confused. However, He reassured them that His Father would send "another Encourager" to comfort, counsel, and teach them after He had departed from this earth. Jesus called this Encourager the Spirit of Truth.

The Coming of the Holy Spirit

After Christ's death, resurrection, and ascension, the 11 apostles and a small group of disciples—"numbering about 120" (Acts 1:15)—waited in Jerusalem for the Holy Spirit to come, as Jesus had instructed them (v. 4). Their meeting place was probably the same "Upper Room" where Jesus had met with them previously and promised them the Holy Spirit (v. 13). As always, God kept His promise. The Holy Spirit came.

The event was so dramatic and phenomenal that it soon became known all over Jerusalem. Luke records that "suddenly a sound like the blowing of a violent wind came from heaven and filled the whole house where they were sitting. They saw what seemed to be tongues of fire that separated and came to rest on each of them." Furthermore, they "began to speak in other tongues as the Spirit enabled them" (2:2-4).

All of this happened on the Day of Pentecost, which was the final day of a 50-day period when God-fearing Jews gathered from all over the New Testament world to celebrate God's goodness to them (vv. 5-11). And on this specific day the Holy Spirit came!

And then the apostles began to understand more fully what Jesus had been teaching them.

The Second Coming of Christ

One point, however, was not clear. The apostles did not understand God's timetable regarding Jesus Christ's return to earth. In fact, the last word they had received was that spoken by the "two men dressed in white" who "stood beside them" after Jesus had been "taken up before their very eyes" (1:9-10). " 'Men of Galilee,' they said, 'why do you stand here looking into the sky? This same Jesus, who has been taken from you into heaven, will come back in the same way you have seen Him go into heaven' " (v. 11).

From their limited perspective, and without more specific information, they could only conclude that Jesus might return very quickly. Had He not told them earlier that He was going away to prepare a place for them and that He would return to take them to be with Him? (John 14:1-3)

If you had come from a distant place, what would you have done? After all, you had already been in Jerusalem for at least 50 days. Personally, you couldn't have gotten me out of Jerusalem with a log chain and a Mac Truck. I would have stayed for what I believed was the next great event—Christ's return.

Evidently this is what the great majority of Jewish believers did. Even those who lived in Jerusalem and the small towns nearby began preparing themselves for that great day. They opened their hearts and homes to their fellow Jews who had come from distant places. Some of these people actually sold their "possessions and goods" and "gave to everyone as he had need" (Acts 2:45). After setting up a semi-communal society, many of those from other parts of the New Testament world decided to stay in Jerusalem and wait for Christ to come once again—this time to set up His kingdom on earth.

Obviously, this was not God's plan. In their excitement, the apostles no doubt forgot Jesus' answer to one of their questions. "Lord," they had asked, "are You at this time going to restore the kingdom to Israel?"

Jesus had answered, "It is not for you to know the times or dates the Father has set by His own authority. But you will receive power when the Holy Spirit comes on you; and you will be My witnesses in Jerusalem, and in all Judea and Samaria, and to *the ends of the earth"* (1:7-8).

Had they remembered these words, the apostles probably would have taken more active steps to encourage the visiting Jewish believers to leave Jerusalem and carry the Good News of Christ's death and resurrection back to their own hometowns.

But God, in His sovereign way, once again used evil men to accomplish His divine purpose. Persecution hit Jerusalem with great force and Christians were scattered everywhere. But they "preached the Word wherever they went" (8:4). This began the great process of evangelism that has continued for nearly 2,000 years. And since that time, Christians who know and understand and believe the Scriptures are still waiting expectantly for Christ to return. We realize that "the Lord is not slow in keeping His promises." Rather, "He is patient . . . not wanting anyone to perish, but everyone to come to repentance" (2 Peter 3:9).

An Unselfish Act of Love (Acts 4:32-35)

Against this historical backdrop, we can better understand Barnabas and why the apostles called him "Son of Encouragement." When he stepped on stage in the Book of Acts, we read that "all the believers were one in heart and mind. No one claimed that any of his possessions was his own, but they shared everything they had . . . there were no needy persons among them. For from time to time those who owned lands or houses sold them, brought the money from the sales and put it at the apostles' feet, and it was distributed to anyone as he had need" (Acts 4:32-35).

One Christian who sold his personal property and gave the proceeds to be distributed to the needy was Barnabas. Originally Barnabas was from Cyprus, though obviously he now lived in Jerusalem where he owned land. When money was needed, he "sold a field he owned and brought the money and put it at the apostles' feet" (v. 37).

Originally this man's name was Joseph. But the apostles changed his name to Barnabas—even before this event. Clearly, this Christian was so outstanding that God's appointed leaders changed his name to match his lifestyle. He was already known in Jerusalem as a Christian who evidently went beyond the call of duty to encourage other believers.

What This Passage Does Not Mean

First, this passage does not teach that Christians today should set up a communal society, and pool their resources to distribute the proceeds equally to the needy. In fact, this plan did not continue even in the New Testament world. It was discontinued when persecution scattered the believers. Furthermore, even in Jerusalem the plan was purely voluntary. Not every Christian took part. Christians who did sold their property when the need arose (4:34), but only as they purposed in their own hearts to do so (5:4).

We should understand, however, that there may be occasions in history when this kind of plan may be proper and necessary. Christians certainly have the freedom to be involved in this kind of societal arrangement. But it is also true that this is not God's normal plan for economic survival. In fact, the only time that it was practiced in the New Testament world was in the early days of the church in the city of Jerusalem.

Secondly, this passage does not teach that spiritual unity depends on *economic equality.* Though their willingness to share everything certainly contributed to their oneness of heart and mind, those New Testament believers had a far deeper cause of their unity—their *equality in Christ* and *love for one another.* As Paul wrote later to the Galatians, "There is neither Jew nor Greek, slave nor free, male nor female, for you are all one in Christ Jesus" (Gal. 3:28).

What This Passage Does Mean

In future chapters we'll see that Barnabas had many qualities that caused the apostles to call him Son of Encouragement. But notice that the first major event recorded about Barnabas was that he "sold a field he owned and brought the money and put it at the apostles' feet" (Acts 4:37).

Why would the Holy Spirit be so specific? Why didn't He just have Luke record that Barnabas was simply a generous man? Shouldn't references to money and what Christians give specifically be a private matter? Didn't the Lord know He might hurt someone's feelings who was not able to do what Barnabas did? And didn't the apostles know that they might hurt somebody if they called Barnabas "Son of Encouragement" and not someone else? Or might not this action on their part cause some other Christians to do the same thing with improper motives?

The answers to these questions seem rather obvious. The Holy Spirit wanted Barnabas to be a model to us all—a specific model. Christians who share their material possessions with others in order to meet human needs and to do God's work have a special ministry of encouragement. In fact, there may be no act of love that is more encouraging. After all, when we share material possessions we are sharing an important part of ourselves. In many respects, it is the true test of our love for Jesus Christ and His work on earth.

Charles Ryrie in his book, *Balancing the Christian Life,* spoke about this issue. He wrote:

> To be sure, a vital spiritual life is related to fellowship with the Lord in His Word and prayer, and to service for the Lord in His work. But our love for God may be proved by something that is a major part of everyone's life, and that is our use of money. How we use our money demonstrates the reality of our love for God. In some ways it proves our love more consciously than depth of knowledge, length of prayers, or prominence of service. Those things can be feigned, but the use of our possessions shows us up for what we actually are (Moody Press, p. 84).

Specific Lessons for 20th-Century Christians

From Act I in Barnabas' life, we see that Christians who share their material possessions are—in a special way—encouragers. Not only do they make others feel happy and good, but their acts of love encourage others to do the same.

Furthermore, people who are faithful in sharing their material possessions deserve special recognition, though obviously this must be done sensitively, and not necessarily in a public way. In fact, most Christians prefer private recognition to public recognition. But, as they are recognized and appreciated in some way, they themselves are encouraged.

There are, however, some *specific* lessons we can learn from this passage and from Barnabas' example. Let's look at four of them.

1. As a Christian, am I characterized more by unselfishness than selfishness? Undergirding Barnabas' act of sacrifice and love was a basic Christian attitude—unselfishness. We'll see this even more clearly as we study more of his life. He was more concerned about others than himself.

Unselfish Christians are automatically encouraging to others. They go out of their way to meet other's needs. They are sensitive to human problems and concerns. They're not so wrapped up in themselves that they cannot see beyond their own needs. They're looking for opportunities to encourage.

If we are to become Christians who share ourselves and our possessions with others, we must deal with these deeper questions. *What is my heart really like? Do I really care about others more than myself?* As we become unselfish our material gifts and other acts of love become acceptable to God and encouraging to others.

2. *To what extent do I encourage my spiritual leaders?* It is significant that the Holy Spirit guided Luke to record that the *apostles* changed Joseph's name to Barnabas, and then specifically told us what that name meant. As spiritual leaders, the apostles were encouraged by Barnabas' spirit of sacrificial giving.

Any Christian leader who directs a ministry can identify with the apostles' feelings. Along with leadership always goes the responsibility for financial management—raising money, paying salaries, supporting missionaries, and caring for other expenses. And when God's people respond—particularly without being coerced—it becomes an encouraging experience. That's what happened in Jerusalem.

People who know me well, know that I can get really excited about a lot of things. Positive results of any kind fill my days with sunshine. But, I must admit, the one thing that encourages me most is when God's people are faithful financial stewards.

One day I was talking with a fellow pastor in Dallas. His congregation had sold their original facility and were planning to construct a new building in another location. They spotted 15 acres they wanted, but the land was owned by a well-known Christian doctor. Representatives from the church offered the doctor $5,000 per acre. He promised to consider their offer.

In the meantime the doctor began to investigate the church—who these people were, what they believed, etc. After careful prayer and thought, he called those people back and reported that they could have the property—not for $5,000 per acre—but for *nothing!* He was donating his land to the church!

Do you think my pastor friend and those people were encouraged? You bet they were—and so was I! Here was a modern-day Barnabas.

Remember, however, that the amount given does not determine the "measure of encouragement." Though sizeable sums do encourage us all because of what can be done, there is also special encouragement when a Christian gives a small gift, but gives it sacrificially. In some cases, it may represent *greater* sacrifice than the one who gives a large gift. This is why the Lord Jesus was so impressed with the widow's mites (Luke 21:1-4).

3. Am I seeking first the kingdom of God? When Jesus delivered His Sermon on the Mount, He spoke directly about what our perspective should be regarding our material possessions. "Do not store up for yourselves treasures on earth, where moth and rust destroy, and where thieves break in and steal. But store up for yourselves treasures in heaven, where moth and rust do not destroy, and where thieves do not break in and steal. For where your treasure is, there your heart will be also" (Matt. 6:19-21).

Jesus then put it all together in one statement as He concluded His teachings on this subject: "But seek first His kingdom and His righteousness; and all these things will be given to you as well" (v. 33).

We are living in an inflationary culture, which is not new in history (even in U.S. history). But the kind of inflation we face now *is* rather new to most people who are less than 50 years old. Inflation *always* creates financial pressure. What happens when you begin to feel financial strain—when your income does not keep up with rising costs? What do you cut from your budget first? The easiest to cut is your giving for God's work.

I challenge you to always take Jesus' statements seriously. Rather than cutting back on what you give the Lord, if at all possible, increase it. Step out by faith and trust Him. I guarantee—on the authority of Scriptures—that He will honor your faithfulness—*if* you keep your motives in proper perspective. And this leads to the final question.

4. *Are my motives proper?* There's a sobering story that follows the account of what Barnabas did. Ananias and Sapphira saw what was happening—how people were selling their property and bringing the money to the apostles to be distributed among the people. Together they conspired to try to make a good impression. They too sold a piece of property. They decided to bring only part of the money, but gave the impression that they had brought it all.

What happened was quite stunning. Both Ananias and Sapphira were struck dead—not because they kept back part of the money—but because they tried to give people the impression that they had given it all. Peter made this point very clear. "Didn't it belong to you before it was sold? After it was sold, wasn't the money at your disposal? What made you think of doing such a thing? You have not lied to men, but to God" (Acts 5:4).

This story is indeed sobering. Fortunately, God rarely deals with people in this way. If He did, I'd probably be one of the first to fall over dead—for God knows that my motives have not always been above reproach.

You see, Ananias and Sapphira purposely lied to the Holy Spirit in the light of God's full revelation of Himself through dynamic miracles, signs, and wonders. In those days God spoke directly to people through the apostles and other selected leaders. They were more responsible before God at that moment because of the light they had.

But I also believe the lesson is clear for all of us. God wants pure motives and honesty. On the one hand, Barnabas was publicly honored by the apostles because of what he did—with pure motives. Ananias and Sapphira were punished because they tried to do the same thing, but lied in the process.

The principle is clear. God wants our love. He wants honesty. He wants us to give, but He wants us to give with proper motives.

A Prayer Response

Lord, help me to be a Barnabas. May I continually encourage others by being a good steward of what You have given me. May I be a good example to my children and to other members of my larger family—the body of Christ. Help me to always seek Your kingdom first, trusting that You'll meet my needs accordingly. And may my motives always be right and proper. May I not give to get, but rather to honor You and to encourage others. Amen.

4

Barnabas—Son of Encouragement, Act II

Scene I—The City of Jerusalem

As the church grew and expanded its influence in Jerusalem, widespread persecution soon hit with full force. In its initial stages, it was precipitated primarily by jealousy on the part of some of the Jewish religious leaders and was directed at the apostles (Acts 5: 17-18). But as more and more Jews accepted Jesus Christ as their true Messiah and joined the new company of Christians, more and more leaders became threatened and angry.

The martyrdom of Stephen was the event that opened the floodgates and launched an all-out wave of persecution against the church. Stephen stood before the Sanhedrin, which involved the full assembly of the elders of Israel. He bore a strong and dynamic witness to the fact that Jesus Christ was indeed the promised Messiah.

Intensely humiliated and angered by his indictment against them for rejecting and crucifying the Son of God, "they all rushed at him, dragged him out of the city, and began to stone him" (7:57-58).

In the midst of those who committed this horrible crime was a young and zealous Pharisee named Saul. Sincerely believing he was doing God a service by trying to stop the spread of Christianity, he approved of Stephen's martyrdom (7:58—8:1). Luke records it was "on that day a great persecution broke out against the church at Jerusalem, and all except the apostles were scattered throughout Judea and Samaria" (8:1).

42

From that point forward, Saul emerged as the primary leader in organizing and furthering the persecution. Waging outright war against believers in Jerusalem, he was determined to stamp out what he considered a false religion. "Going from house to house, he dragged off men and women and put them in prison" (v. 3).

Scene II—The Road to Damascus (Acts 9:1-9)

Saul's efforts in Jerusalem were so successful he resolved to expand them. He "went to the high priest and asked him for letters to the synagogues in Damascus, so that if he found any there who belonged to the Way, whether men or women, he might take them as prisoners to Jerusalem" (9:2).

Granted his desire, Saul headed toward Damascus, accompanied by a group of men. As he neared the city, "suddenly a light from heaven flashed around him." Luke records that he heard a voice saying, "Saul, Saul, why do you persecute Me?" (vv. 3-4)

The voice was that of Jesus Christ Himself. Stunned and struck blind, Saul fell to the ground. We read that the "men traveling with Saul stood there speechless" (vv. 5-7). And when Saul stood up, the men with him had to lead him by the hand into Damascus.

Scene III—The City of Damascus (Acts 9:10-25)

In Damascus the Lord had prepared a man, Ananias, to minister to Saul (9:10-12). Understandably, Ananias was frightened when the Lord spoke to him and asked him to seek out Saul. "Lord," he responded, "I have heard many reports about this man and all the harm he has done to Your saints in Jerusalem. And he has come here with authority from the chief priests to arrest all who call on Your name" (vv. 13-14).

However, the Lord reassured Ananias that he had nothing to fear. Saul was now a different man—a converted man. Perhaps more dramatic than Saul's conversion itself was the fact that God told Ananias He had chosen this man to carry His "name before the Gentiles and their kings and before the people of Israel" (v. 15).

Ananias obeyed the Lord. He found Saul, ministered to him, and reassured him of God's hand on his life. Saul's response was immediate. He was baptized, signifying his new allegiance. After spending "several days with the disciples in Damascus," he immediately "began to preach in the synagogues that Jesus is the Son of God" (vv. 19-20).

People who heard Saul couldn't believe their ears—or eyes. Here was the man who had jailed numerous Christians and had threatened them with death, now preaching the very message he had rejected. No wonder many questioned his sincerity and thought this was simply an insidious way to achieve his original goals.

But if there were doubts about his true conversion, they were soon dispelled by his effectiveness as a Christian evangelist. Saul's forceful personality was just as evident as a zealous Christian as it had been as a zealous Jew. Once he was converted he was just as forceful *for Christ* as he had been *against Christ*. In fact, he was so powerful in his witness that he "baffled the Jews living in Damascus by proving that Jesus is the Christ" (v. 22).

Ironically, the tables were eventually turned on Saul. So threatened were the Jews, that they conspired to kill him for preaching the same message he himself had tried to stamp out. But with the help of fellow Christians who had become his friends, Saul escaped from Damascus. His enemies had set up a guard day and night at the "city gates in order to kill him" should he try to leave Damascus. But one night, his friends "lowered him in a basket through an opening in the wall" and he escaped unharmed (vv.24-25).

Scene IV—Return to Jerusalem (Acts 9:26-30)

It is easy to imagine what the disciples thought when they heard that Saul, the persecutor, had returned to Jerusalem. When he tried to join the Christians he had attempted to jail and even murder, they were understandably frightened.

It was then that Barnabas once again entered the scene—demonstrating his encouraging qualities. When all of the believers in Jerusalem distrusted and rejected Saul, we read that "Barnabas took him and brought him to the apostles." There he laid out the facts one by one regarding Saul's conversion to Christ and his new lifestyle. First, "he told them how Saul on his journey had seen the Lord"; secondly he told them how "the Lord had spoken to him"; thirdly Barnabas reported "how in Damascus [Saul] had preached fearlessly in the name of Jesus," the name he used to hate so desperately (9:27).

It is understandable why Saul needed someone to verify his sincerity and the reality of his Christian experience. There have always been people in the world who have feigned conversion for some kind of personal gain.

I'm reminded of Chuck Colson, Richard Nixon's close assistant during his presidential campaign as well as during his years in office. Mr. Colson was often ruthless in his dealings with people and was frequently referred to as Nixon's "hatchet man," the one who handled the President's "dirty work." One person described Mr. Colson in the press by saying he "would walk over his own grandmother if he had to."

It is not surprising that when Chuck Colson became a Christian and confessed his wrongdoings, many people doubted his sincerity. After he served his jail term and began his ministry, many Christians were skeptical. If it were not for those who knew firsthand the reality of his Christian experience, and who were willing to play a "Barnabas role" in bearing witness to that fact, Mr. Colson would have had a difficult time convincing people he was indeed a different man—a converted man.

In Jerusalem this was Saul's dilemma. Saul had developed a reputation as a ruthless persecutor of Christians. But thanks to Barnabas, his true conversion to Christianity was verified. The apostles were convinced, for we read that "Saul stayed with them and moved about freely in Jerusalem, speaking boldly in the name of the Lord" (v. 28).

Eventually, however, Saul also faced serious problems in Jerusalem, just as he had in Damascus. Because of his strong witness to his fellow Jews, some of them tried to take his life. Consequently, he had to leave Jerusalem, ending up in Tarsus (vv. 29-30).

Some Observations

Though most of this story revolves around Saul's experience as a zealous Jew and then as a zealous Christian, another man stands out once again in the stage of New Testament history. He is Barnabas—Son of Encouragement. Though his appearance is stated only briefly in Luke's account, his influence at that moment was profound. He served as the bridge between the men who were called to be apostles while Christ was on earth and the man who was called to be an apostle after Christ had returned to heaven.

And Saul—later called Paul—was to become one of the greatest apostles and missionaries of all time.

Why was Barnabas' action so important? First, it helps us better understand why the apostles changed his name. Originally called Joseph, they gave him a new name because he was well-known for his *encouraging* activities (4:36). And he willingly shared his material goods with those in need. He was an *unselfish* man.

In Acts 9 we see a second reason why Barnabas was an encourager. *He had a basic concern for people, particularly when they were being rejected by others. He was willing to trust them when others did not.* The circumstances surrounding Barnabas' support of Saul in Jerusalem illustrated dramatically the depth of this quality in his life.

1. Barnabas' actions were rooted in unselfishness. Barnabas' willingness to help Saul was in itself an extension of his *unselfish spirit.* He no doubt had enough problems and pressures in the ministry without getting involved so deeply in Saul's life. Furthermore, he knew he was putting his own reputation on the line. But he saw a man in need—a man he believed was sincere—and he knew he could help.

Of course Barnabas did not naively trust Saul. His trust was based on facts. This is obvious from what Barnabas said to the apostles about Saul's conversion and subsequent actions (9:27). He knew what had happened to Saul because he took the time to find out. How easy it would have been to judge Saul's situation without making an effort to really discover the truth. This only verifies the fact that Barnabas was willing to get involved in other people's lives—to find out what was really true—and then to act on that truth.

Remember, however, that all the facts in the world still call for an element of trust. People are unpredictable and can change directions in midstream. They can let you down. But despite this possibility, Barnabas was willing to believe in Saul—primarily because he believed in people. He did not allow the exceptions to disillusion him and destroy his capacity to trust.

2. Barnabas' actions revealed a willingness to become vulnerable. Barnabas believed in Saul when almost everyone else— including the apostles—questioned his sincerity. Imagine the public and personal pressure on Barnabas. After all, he was representing a murderer—a man who had approved of Stephen's death and had launched an unmerciful attack against the church in Jerusalem. How easy and emotionally comfortable it would have been to remain silent.

But not Barnabas! He went right to the top, asked for an audience with the apostles and stated why he believed in Saul. Barnabas was more concerned for Saul and the Lord's work than for his own feelings and comfortable existence. In short, this is unselfishness personified.

3. Barnabas' attitudes and actions in Jerusalem were a consistent part of his life. Another incident involving Barnabas helps show that his willingness to believe in people was indeed a consistent part of his Christian character.

Several years after this defense of Saul, Saul and Barnabas were called by the Holy Spirit to serve together as a missionary team. A young man named John Mark traveled with them as "their helper" (13:1-5). However, a short time after they began their evangelistic tour—when the going got tough—"John left them to return to Jerusalem" (v. 13). Consequently, Saul and Barnabas completed the trip without him.

Sometime later, Saul and Barnabas agreed to return to the newly established churches and offer any needed advice or encouragement. Barnabas suggested that they once again take John Mark. But Saul (now called Paul) balked at the idea. Paul "did not think it wise to take him, because he had deserted them in Pamphylia and had not continued with them in the work." In fact, Barnabas and Paul "had such a sharp disagreement that they parted company." Barnabas took Mark and sailed for Cyprus, but Paul chose Silas—and they "went through Syria and Cilicia, strengthening the churches" (15:36-41).

How ironic! Several years earlier Barnabas had believed in Paul and represented him before the apostles in Jerusalem. Now we see Barnabas confronting Paul on behalf of John Mark.

Who was right and who was wrong in this incident? I'm not sure we can say absolutely. But if I had to make a choice, I would have to go with Barnabas—for he wanted to give John Mark another chance. If he had not, who knows what may have happened to this young man. John Mark may have become so discouraged that he may never have again attempted anything for God. But he did try again. In fact, the Holy Spirit chose him along with Mat-

thew, Luke, and the Apostle John to write one of the Gospels—
the Gospel of Mark.

Much later, shortly before Paul's death, he recognized and
acknowledged Mark's significant contribution to the ministry when he wrote to Timothy. "Get Mark and bring him
with you, because he is helpful to me in my ministry"
(2 Tim. 4:11).

The point is clear. Barnabas *believed* in people! He believed in
Paul when he was rejected by the Christians in Jerusalem. Later
he believed in John Mark when he was rejected by Paul. There's
no doubt that this quality was a consistent part of Barnabas' life
and that is another reason why he was called Son of Encouragement.

A Psychological Insight

Barnabas exemplified Jesus Christ in his willingness to believe
in people and to act on that belief by helping them, even when
it cost him personally. After all, "While we were still sinners
Christ died for us" (Rom. 5:8). The Apostle John wrote, "This
is how we know what love is: Jesus Christ laid down His life
for us. And we ought to lay down our lives for our brothers"
(1 John 3:16).

But there may be another reason why Barnabas was so sensitive
to people. Though this observation is purely speculative, some
believe it is quite feasible. When the apostles met together after
Christ had returned to heaven to determine who would replace
Judas, there were two candidates: one was Joseph, called Barsabbas; the other was Mathias. When they drew lots, Mathias was
chosen (Acts 1:23-26).

Why is that significant? For this reason: Some believe that
Joseph called *Barsabbas* may also have been *Joseph,* whose
name was later changed by the apostles to *Barnabas.* If this is
true—and it is quite possible that it is—perhaps we can understand why Barnabas was so sensitive to people who were
rejected. He knew firsthand the emotional pain that comes
to all of us at times. Consequently, Barnabas could identify with others who were going through the same experience.

But if this observation is valid, it also reflects even more
significantly on the depth of this man's Christian character. Rather

than becoming bitter, he became more sensitive, more spiritual, more committed to believing in people. How easy it would have been for him to harbor resentment and to vent that resentment by siding with the apostles against Paul, rather than standing up for him when the apostles were questioning the sincerity of his conversion.

Rejection and its accompanying pain can drive us in one of two directions. We can spend our lives looking for ways to get even—and vent our anger on both guilty and innocent people—particularly in situations that are similar to our own bad experiences. Or, we can learn from the experience and commit our lives to helping and encouraging others who may be experiencing the same difficulties. This may indeed have been a motivating factor in the life of Barnabas.

Barnabas and You

What specific lessons can a 20th-century Christian learn from these events in the life of Barnabas?

1. Our hesitancy to trust others and to defend them may relate to the fact that we are dealing with untrustworthy people.

This is always a possibility. There are people whom we have difficulty trusting and recommending to others because they have let us down so often. Though they may try to reassure us that they are trustworthy, we have to see some evidence of change before we can feel free to trust them again.

Bob had this kind of experience with Jack. Bob trusted Jack implicitly. He backed him, promoted him, encouraged him. In fact, Bob was responsible for getting Jack his job. Later he discovered that Jack had denied that Bob had anything to do with his position. Jack was saying negative things about Bob behind his back in order to build up his own reputation.

Then one day Jack's kingdom collapsed. Eventually the true facts came to the surface and Bob was vindicated.

This experience teaches us several lessons. We must not let a bad experience keep us from trusting people. Even in difficult situations—if we do not take matters into our own hands and try to get even—God will eventually vindicate us. When God vindicates us, there is no better vindication!

We must remember that people such as Bob and Jack are the exception, not the rule. Most Christians *are* trustworthy. In fact, most people's actions correspond directly to the amount of trust we place in them. This leads to the conclusion that many of the difficulties we have in trusting people focus on *us*—not on others.

2. *We have difficulty trusting people because we are unwilling to spend time getting involved in their lives.* It is much easier to travel in our own little worlds, doing our "own things." Barnabas could have easily taken this route, but he didn't. He took time to get the facts and then to "build bridges" for Saul.

How easy it is to say negative things about people when we don't know the facts. Since we have nothing to say, we say something negative, which is often based on "old" but untrue information. We must remember that people *do* change. Our responsibility as Christians—if we're going to make a statement—is to find out what is indeed true.

3. *At times we do not convey our trust in people because we are fearful of the majority who do not agree with us.* We must remember that the majority may *not* have the facts. If *we* do, we are responsible before God and other Christians to let these facts be known. This is what Barnabas did and it changed the understanding and attitude of the majority.

4. *We may fail to stand up for others and communicate our trust because we fear rejection from key people we love and trust.* Barnabas certainly must have felt this when he confronted Paul —a best friend—regarding John Mark. This was a true test of his character and concern for others. This must be our motivation when we are tempted not to trust someone and let it be known because we fear rejection from a close friend or associate.

5. *We may not trust people because we are unwilling to take a risk.* Risk is always involved. People, no matter how sincere they are, will fail and occasionally let us down. Though our own public image may be somewhat involved, it is far better to become *known* as a trusting person than one who is always skeptical of others. For if we become known as untrusting people, we will in turn not be trusted. Our relationships with others will deteriorate.

6. *We may not trust others because we have been hurt and rejected ourselves.* Consequently, we go through life punishing others. On the other hand, we can become more sensitive to people because of our difficult experiences. We can become

"encouragers" from the "inside out" because we know what it feels like not to be trusted.

Life Response

Think of one person you can encourage by demonstrating your trust. If you have difficulty demonstrating your trust and letting that person and others know about it, use the preceding statements to honestly try to understand *why*. Then make an effort to overcome the difficulty—no matter what the problem may be.

5

Barnabas—Son of Encouragement, Act III

Setting the Stage—A Historical Sketch

There was a time in the history of the world that *all* men and women turned away from God. In fact, they turned *against* God! Paul described this dismal situation in his letter to the Romans. "For although they knew God, they neither glorified Him as God nor gave thanks to Him, but their thinking became futile and their foolish hearts were darkened" (Rom. 1:21).

During this time of human deterioration, people actually "exchanged the glory of the immortal God for images made to look like mortal man and *birds* and *animals* and *reptiles*" (v. 23). Their spiritual and moral deterioration is obvious in Paul's record. They moved from worshiping God to worshiping man and then to lower forms of animals.

But God in His mercy did not turn His back on mankind though people turned their backs on God. He reached down in love and chose first, a man (Abraham), and then a nation (Israel) through whom He would reveal His love and draw many people back to Himself. This is why we call the Jews God's "chosen people"— chosen, not because God shows favoritism, but because He chose them to be the channel through whom He would reveal His righteousness and holiness and eventually His Son, Jesus Christ, to be the Saviour of the world (2:9-11).

Jesus Christ was born as a Jew. His parents, Joseph and Mary, were of the tribe of Judah. As Jesus began His public ministry, He naturally chose 12 Jewish men to be His apostles and missionaries.

Since the Jews are those people who had become recipients of God's laws, they became Christ's first target audience for His message of grace and truth.

After Jesus' return to heaven, the Holy Spirit came first upon those Jews who responded to Christ's message that He was indeed the Messiah. As they began to share the Good News of Christ's death and resurrection, they naturally communicated this message to their fellow Jews. Consequently, the first church—the church in Jerusalem—was a Jewish church.

However, these first-century Christians had a theological problem. Though what they believed about Jesus Christ was indeed accurate, their view of who could be saved was inaccurate. In fact, some were so nationally oriented in their thinking that they actually believed that only Jews could become true followers of Christ.

From a human point of view, all of this is understandable. Though God made it clear all along in His written revelation that "all peoples of the earth" would "be blessed" through the Jewish race (Gen. 12:1-3), the Jews lost sight of both their earthly and heavenly purpose. Even the 12 apostles didn't understand Christ's words to them when He said, "I have other sheep [Gentiles] that are not of this sheep pen [Israel]. I must bring them also. They too will listen to My voice, and there shall be *one flock* and *one Shepherd*" (John 10:16).

Against this historical backdrop we can understand more clearly the transition these first-century Jews faced. They had to accept the fact that God's salvation in Christ was available to all mankind. No scene is more dramatic than that experience which convinced the Apostle Peter that the Gospel was for Gentiles as well as Jews.

Scene I—Peter's Second Conversion
(Acts 10:1—11:18)

One day Peter went up to pray on the roof of the house where he was staying. During this time of prayer, he "became hungry." While a meal was being prepared down below, he "fell into a trance" and saw a most unusual vision. Heaven opened and a large sheet descended, held by its four corners, and filled with all kinds of animals. Then Peter heard a voice: "Get up, Peter. Kill and eat" (Acts 10:13).

Peter resisted since, *as a Jew,* he had *never* eaten any animals classified in the law as "unclean"—and the sheet included some of those animals. But three times the voice instructed Peter to eat and not to "call anything impure that God had made clean" (v. 15).

Peter couldn't understand what was happening. But in the meantime God had spoken to Cornelius, *a Gentile,* who lived in Caesarea. Cornelius had been worshiping God and seeking to do His will. One afternoon, he too had a vision. An angel of the Lord appeared to him and told him to look for Peter in Joppa.

To make a long story short, Cornelius sent three men to find Peter. When they arrived in Joppa, Peter's heart had been prepared through his own vision. The next day he traveled to Caesarea with the men to meet with Cornelius and his family. When Peter heard Cornelius' full story, he took a great step forward in understanding and accepting God's redemptive plan of salvation. He told Cornelius, "I now realize how true it is that God *does not show favoritism,* but accepts men from every nation who fear Him and do what is right. This is the message God sent to the people of Israel, telling the good news of peace through Jesus Christ, who is *Lord of all"* (vv. 34-36).

Peter had *heard* this truth before (from the lips of Christ Himself). But he seemingly did not believe it or accept it in his heart. He was a staunch and prejudiced Jew who had been saturated with Hebrew tradition. As with Saul, it took a dramatic event, a revelation of God, and for Peter a *"second* conversion," to convince him that God cared about Gentiles and had provided for their salvation.

But God, in His mercy and grace, was also working in the hearts of other Jews, which leads to our next scene.

Scene II—The Church in Antioch (Acts 11:19-21)

Luke's historical record speaks for itself. We read, "Now those who had been scattered by the persecution in connection with Stephen traveled as far as Phoenicia, Cyprus, and Antioch, telling the message *only to the Jews."*

It's clear from this statement that Jewish prejudice among these first-century Christians was rather pervasive. But there were some who were more open-minded—particularly those who had lived in parts of the New Testament world where they rubbed shoulders daily with Gentiles. Thus we read that some of the Jews from Cyprus and Cyrene, who had been visiting in Jerusalem on the day of Pentecost, "went to Antioch and began to speak to *Greeks also,* telling them the Good News about the Lord Jesus." The results? We read that "the Lord's hand was with them, and a great number of people believed and turned to the Lord" (11:20-21).

Scene III—Barnabas Sent to Antioch (Acts 11:22-24)

What was happening in Antioch soon "reached the ears of the church in Jerusalem" (11:22). Providentially, God had already prepared the Jerusalem Christians for this news through Peter's encounter with Cornelius. After Peter's dramatic experience, he returned to Jerusalem and shared what had happened. Though some in the church were hard to convince, they eventually "had no further objections and praised God, saying, 'So then, God has *even granted the Gentiles* repentance unto life'" (v. 18). Though this statement reflects what they actually thought of Gentiles, they were beginning to understand the dimensions of God's grace.

The depth of their understanding is seen in their sense of responsibility to send someone to Antioch to help nurture the new Gentile Christians. Once again Barnabas, Son of Encouragement, entered the scene. The believers in Jerusalem chose him to carry out this mission. "When he arrived and saw the evidence of the grace of God, he was glad and *encouraged them all* to remain true to the Lord with all their hearts" (v. 23).

Some Observations

Once again an exciting story ends *and* begins with the focus on Barnabas. Though he enters the action in the final scene, he stands out as a lead character in God's dealings with Gentiles.

Why was Barnabas chosen for this task?

1. First, Barnabas had developed a reputation in the Christian world as an "encourager"—a man who was deeply concerned for people and who could get excited about progress in others' lives. We can speculate that it didn't take the apostles and other Jerusalem Christians long to conclude who was suited to handle this difficult missionary task. Barnabas had clearly demonstrated his trustworthiness and his positive nature. Note that when he arrived in

Antioch and saw that God had really done a special work in these people's hearts *"he was glad"* (11:23).

Why would the Holy Spirit lead Luke to record Barnabas' *emotional* response to what he saw in Antioch? It seems clear that this was just another reason why this man was called Barnabas—Son of Encouragement. He got excited about the ministry, about people, and about what God was doing in their lives.

I believe that Barnabas had his own kind of personal magnetism. His positive attitude was contagious and encouraging to others, particularly to those who tended to get discouraged and downhearted. Though this is purely speculation, it certainly correlates with what we've already learned about this man. No person is more encouraging than one who can get excited about what is happening in the lives of others.

2. *A second reason they sent Barnabas to Antioch was because of his spiritual qualifications.* Luke clearly specifies that "he was a good man, full of the Holy Spirit and faith" (v. 24). Barnabas stands out as a man especially gifted by the Lord for this kind of task and also as a man who was living what he believed and taught. This is also clear from what he did when he arrived in Antioch. He "encouraged them all to remain true to the Lord with all their hearts" (v. 23).

It is hard to encourage others to do something we have not done ourselves. Consequently, we can safely conclude that Barnabas was also a man who remained true to the Lord with all *his heart.* Following Christ and living for Him was no sideline with Barnabas. He put the Lord first in everything. Christianity *was* his life.

The Apostle Paul and his co-workers Timothy and Silas also practiced what they preached. They earned the right to "encourage others to remain true to the Lord" by demonstrating that quality in their own lives. Thus Paul wrote to the Thessalonians, reflecting on his ministry among them, "You are witnesses, and so is God, of how holy, righteous and blameless we were among you who believed. For you know that we dealt with each of you as a father deals with his own children, *encouraging,* comforting, and urging you *to live lives worthy of God"* (1 Thes. 2:10-12).

3. A third reason the church in Jerusalem sent Barnabas to Antioch was that he may have been more free from prejudice than others. There are some natural explanations for this possibility. First, Barnabas was originally a resident of Cyprus (Acts 4:36). It is certainly significant that it was "men from Cyprus" who first preached the Gospel in Antioch. Perhaps Barnabas was chosen for this task because he understood the Gentile mindset and culture better than others. It is even possible that it may been some of his friends who had won believers in Antioch to Christ.

But it is also possible that Barnabas was more free from prejudice than those who lived most of their lives in an exclusively Jewish culture. This too may illustrate why he was such an encouraging person. He may have found it easy to accept people as people—not because of their heritage and cultural backgrounds, but because they too were made in God's image.

Barnabas and You

What kind of Christian am I? What kind of Christian are you? How do we measure up to the qualifications that made Barnabas the kind of man who could be trusted with this kind of Christian responsibility?

Note! Though we may never be called on to handle this kind of heavy missionary task, we nevertheless should reflect the same qualities in our own Christian environment.

1. Christians should encourage others by entering into others' lives enthusiastically. Barnabas was that kind of man. He got excited when other Christians made spiritual progress.

When I became a Christian, several other Christians let me know *how glad* they were for me. They went out of their way to show their excitement about my conversion to Christ. Their reactions greatly encouraged me.

Previously, I told you how my life was turned around when a professor at Moody Bible Institute, Dr. Harold Garner, took a personal interest in me. It was important in that process of encouragement that he got excited about what was happening in my life—when I did well on a test, when I taught a good lesson in practice teaching, when I wrote a particularly good paper.

As the years went by, I learned that Dr. Garner demonstrated these attitudes toward many other people. Because he did, he helped change many lives. I know, because without his encouragement I would never have been able to cope with the pressures I faced then. He was indeed an encouraging person. Because of his impact on me, I will never be the same. By God's grace I want to get excited about the good things that happen in other people's lives—and let them know I'm glad. I owe a great debt to this professor, and I feel the best way to repay that debt is to try to encourage others as he encouraged me.

2. *Christians should encourage others with their own Christlike lifestyles.* There's no way we can encourage others effectively—our children, our Christian friends, and others—to "remain true to the Lord with all their hearts" if we aren't true to God ourselves. Like Barnabas, we must exemplify the fruit of the Spirit in our relationships with others—love, joy, peace, patience, kindness, goodness, faithfulness, gentleness, and self-control (Gal. 5:22-23).

Too many Christians today are saying, "Do as I say and not as I do." But we should set Paul's goal as our goal. He was able to write to the Corinthians, "Follow my example as I follow the example of Christ" (1 Cor. 11:1).

A difficult period in my life came early in the ministry. I worked with several Christian leaders whom I admired very much. Through a series of circumstances, they fell out of harmony with each other. They lost trust in each other and they criticized one another privately. To complicate matters, they one by one shared their criticisms of each other with me.

Having struggled to find my own way in life, this was almost too much for me to bear emotionally. I was ready to forget about the ministry and everything I believed. However, something within me would not let me take that step. I poured out my heart before God, though at times I felt my prayers never passed through the ceiling of the room.

One day, someone—and I don't know who—left a book on my desk. The book dealt with the painful experiences that some Christians go through and how God uses those times to equip and prepare His people for a more fruitful ministry. Though I didn't agree with everything I read, God still used that book as a source of light for my troubled soul. It was another turning point in my life.

I learned two great lessons from that experience. First, I must never again depend on people as a primary source of my security and hope. That must come only from Jesus Christ.

But secondly, I learned that God *does* use our consistent Christian lifestyle to encourage others. And by God's grace, I must try to live my life so it would never disillusion others. I've met people who have been hurt by inconsistent Christian living, and the ultimate result has been devastating. We *are* responsible to be examples of Jesus Christ.

3. Christians, of all people, should not be prejudiced. Being prejudiced means forming an opinion or judgment before the facts are known. More specifically, it means to be suspicious and intolerant of people who are different from us.

This was a serious problem in the Jerusalem church. But Barnabas broke away from his provincial attitudes more quickly than others. Consequently, God used him in a very special way.

As I reflect on my own background, I can see how prejudiced I had become because of what I had been taught from childhood. I had grown up in a restrictive and legalistic religious community. For years I had been taught that I was better than other people because of my heritage. All other people who called themselves "Christian" were wrong. I had the truth. No one else did.

Though I rejected those attitudes after I became a true Christian, I did not realize at first how ingrained they were in me. Those prejudiced feelings lingered in my heart. I can see now that God used some of the disillusioning experiences in my life to help me break out of my narrow, provincial, and subtle prejudice. It was only as I was "reaching up to touch bottom" that I realized how much I needed other people who were not from my own religious background.

Prejudice and pride must be dealt with if we are going to be true encouragers of others. We all struggle with this problem. It is only by God's grace that we are what we are. We must realize that "God is no respecter of persons" (Acts 10:34, KJV). His grace and love are for all.

Life Response

To what extent are you "an encouraging Christian"? The following checklist will help you evaluate yourself in this area.

1. Are you able to get excited about the good things that happen to others? Are you able to tell them that you're glad? Can you enter into their joy? If you can, you are an encourager!
2. Are you living a committed Christian life? To what extent are you able to encourage others "to remain true to the Lord with all their hearts"? If you can, you are reflecting your own commitment to Christ. You are an encourager!
3. Are you able to accept other people for who they are? Do you see the best in people? Do you freely associate with people who are different from you? If you can, you are relatively free from prejudice and you are an encourager!

Action Steps

1. Think of one person with whom you have difficulty showing your excitement about successes . . . OR
2. Think of one person you feel you have confused or hurt by some kind of inconsistent Christian behavior . . . OR
3. Think of one person that you have difficulty liking because he is different from you.

Seek out that one person and be a Barnabas in his or her life.

6

Living for Christ in an X-Rated World

After a number of Gentiles in Antioch in Syria believed in Christ, Barnabas was chosen by the Jerusalem believers to go there to encourage these new Christians "to remain true to the Lord with all their hearts" (Acts 11:23). What did Barnabas say and teach? What was the essence of his message of encouragement? To answer these questions adequately, we must understand the culture in which these people lived and we must look at the larger context of the New Testament.

Antioch
Antioch in Syria was the third largest city in the Roman Empire with a population estimated at 500,000 people. It was a luxurious city. Its main street was four miles long and lined with magnificent mansions.

Antioch was a typical pagan city in the Roman Empire, though perhaps more cultured than many. However, its "social life was debased, sensual, and shocking" (Merrill Unger, *Unger's Bible Dictionary*, Moody Press, p. 69). Like Corinth, this kind of licentious lifestyle was accentuated by the fact that it was a seaport city. With time to spend while their boats were being loaded and unloaded, sailors entered into every kind of vice available. Furthermore, "retired government officials spent their fortunes there, surfeiting themselves with its exotic delicacies, gambling their gold coins on the chariot races, and relaxing daily in its great

61

public baths" (*Wycliffe Bible Encyclopedia,* Moody Press, Volume 1, p. 107).

The Church in Antioch

Though a Jewish community had existed in Antioch all along, the city was populated mostly by Gentiles. It was in this city some Jewish men from Cyprus and Cyrene had shared the Gospel with both Greek-speaking Jews and Gentiles, and a number had turned to Jesus Christ. Barnabas' mission was to help these new Christians grow spiritually.

Barnabas faced an unusual challenge. Conversion to Christ did not automatically turn these people into mature Christians. He immediately "encouraged them all to remain true to the Lord with all their hearts" (Acts 11:23).

Barnabas quickly discovered that his ministry in Antioch involved more than nurturing these new Christians. No doubt many of those who were converted brought their relatives and friends to hear Barnabas, for we read that "a great number of people were brought to the Lord" (v. 24).

This growing ministry was more than one man could handle. Consequently, Barnabas probably got up early one morning and headed for Tarsus to look for his friend, Saul. Luke records that "when he found him, he brought him to Antioch. So for a whole year Barnabas and Saul met with the church and taught great numbers of people" (v. 26).

Though we are not told specifically what these men taught and what their ministry was, we are told indirectly. In some respects Luke's subtle journalism, under the guidance of the Holy Spirit, speaks far more potently than direct statements. We simply read, "The disciples were first called Christians at Antioch" (v. 26).

Many believe, as I do, that the unbelieving pagans in Antioch first called the Lord's disciples *Christians.* These new believers began to be so identified with Jesus Christ in their beliefs and lifestyles that they were given a name which reflected this change—for the name Christian means a "follower of Christ."

We are not told exactly what happened to these new Christians—what Paul and Barnabas actually taught them and in what ways they were "encouraged . . . to remain true to the Lord with all their hearts" (v. 23). However, if we review the letters that were written to other churches, we can learn a great deal about what must have happened at Antioch.

We do have one small letter written to the church in Antioch from the apostles and elders in Jerusalem. It is found in Acts 15: 23-29, and the prime exhortation is to "abstain from . . . sexual immorality" (v. 29). However, we do have two comprehensive letters written to churches that were in cities very similar to Antioch in terms of religious and cultural practices. Let's look at the church in Rome and the church in Ephesus.

Rome

When Paul wrote to the church in Rome, the city had not yet reached its pinnacle of growth and success. That would come early in the second century when it would be populated by as many as 1½ million people. But even in Paul's day, Rome was a great city whose influence was felt and admired even beyond the Roman Empire.

Rome, like most cities in the empire, was well-known for its moral degradation. Though not all people in the city took part in the immoral activities, the city was noted for its theaters that featured coarse, cheap humor. The plays dealt with the "lowest kind of life and their presentation was shameless." Dr. Tenney comments further that "the Roman stage degenerated rapidly and contributed directly to the moral degradation of the people" (Merrill C. Tenney, *New Testament Survey,* Eerdmans, pp. 52-53).

In addition to stage shows, the amphitheater contributed significantly to the degeneration of Rome. Contests between men and animals, and men and men provided people with violent and bloody duels that often resulted in death to both men and beasts. In order to cater to a growing appetite for violence, the contests were planned more and more elaborately and became intensely shocking. Again, Dr. Tenney comments: "If the stage with its coarse mimes and farces schooled the populace in obscenity and lust, the gladiatorial shows glorified brutality" (Tenney, *New Testament Survey,* p. 54).

The Church in Rome

At some point during the first century, the Gospel of Jesus Christ penetrated this pagan city. When and how, we do not know. When

Paul wrote his letter to the Romans, he had not yet been there (Rom. 1:10), though he had planned many times to do so (v. 13). He had a strong desire to minister among them and to be encouraged by them (vv. 11-12).

The first part of his letter is doctrinal. He told about what God had done for them, and for all mankind, in Jesus Christ. Though all people have sinned against God (chaps. 1—3), all people—both Jew and Gentile—can be justified in God's sight by grace through faith (chaps. 4—5).

Salvation by grace, however, does not mean Christians should continue to live in sin. Rather than being slaves to sin, we should be slaves to righteousness (chap. 6). Though there is certainly a war in our lives between our old sinful nature and our new nature in Christ (chap. 7), we can have victory by having our "minds set on what the spirit desires" (8:5). All of this, wrote Paul, involves "God's mercy" towards us (12:1)—for in ourselves we are not worthy of this marvelous grace.

Beginning in chapter 12, Paul outlines what a Christian's response should be to God's grace and mercy. *"Therefore,* I urge you, brothers, *in view of God's mercy,* to offer your bodies as living sacrifices" (12:1). The word *urge* comes from the same basic word, *parakaleo,* meaning "to encourage." What Paul is about to say is probably in essence what Barnabas must have said when he encouraged or urged the Christians in Antioch "to remain true to the Lord with all their hearts."

1. "Offer your bodies as living sacrifices, holy and pleasing to God—which is your spiritual worship" (v. 1). These Christians in Rome, particularly the Gentile Christians, were well aware of what Paul was saying. All of their lives they had been giving their bodies over to fulfill fleshly and sensual appetites, either through direct involvement or vicariously in the theaters. They had been living unholy lives, pleasing themselves and and Satan. In reality they were worshiping themselves—not God.

2. "Do not conform any longer to the *pattern of this world"* (v. 2). What the Romans had been doing as non-Christians was no longer to be a part of their Christian lifestyle. The Apostle John made this point even more vivid when he wrote: "Do not love the world or anything in the world. . . . For everything in the world—the cravings of sinful man, the lust of his eyes, and the boasting of what he has and does—comes not from the Father but from the world" (1 John 2:15-16).

3. *"Be transformed by the renewing of your mind.* Then you will be able to test and approve what God's will is—His good, pleasing, and perfect will" (Rom. 12:2). It's obvious from this verse that becoming a mature Christian is a process of becoming more and more conformed to Christ's image. Paul said this would happen as they renewed their minds.

These verses in Romans 12 help us to understand more clearly *how* Barnabas might have *encouraged* the new believers in Antioch "to remain true to the Lord with all their hearts" and what he and Saul taught them during the year they ministered in Antioch. We can only assume that Paul's message remained constant and that the believers in Antioch received the same message as the believers in Rome. But there is another letter that outlines even more completely the content of their message of encouragement.

Ephesus

Ephesus too was a pagan city that was permeated with a Gentile lifestyle. It was the capital of the Roman province of Asia, and was a great trading center, ranking alongside of Antioch. It was also a great pagan religious center, for the temple of Diana, a fertility goddess, was located in Ephesus.

The great temple of Diana was considered one of the seven wonders of the Roman world. An annual festival in Diana's honor was held during the months of March and April. People actually worshiped Diana by means of sensual orgies and ceremonial prostitution. Fathers, mothers, and children observed and took part in these degenerate activities. Multitudes of female virgins were continually initiated as "priestesses" to serve as temple prostitutes.

Ephesus was also a city permeated with occult practices. But "a number who had practiced sorcery brought their scrolls together and burned them publicly. When they calculated the value of the scrolls, the total came to fifty thousand drachmas" (Acts 19:19).

The Church in Ephesus

After the church was founded in Ephesus, Paul stayed for two years and taught regularly in the School of Tyrannus (vv. 8-10). It was here he also *encouraged* these people to "remain true to the Lord with all of their hearts." Later when Paul wrote his letter to these Christians, he spelled out clearly what this involved. In fact, the Ephesian letter is structured much like the Roman letter, and though much shorter, Paul spells out specifically what it meant to turn away from pagan practices.

The first 3 chapters of Paul's letter to the Ephesians are similar to the first 11 chapters of Romans. Paul dealt primarily with God's love and mercy toward Christians. It's in these chapters Paul outlined the great doctrines of Christianity. However, beginning with chapter 4 in the Ephesian letter Paul wrote, "As a prisoner for the Lord, then, I *urge* you to live a life worthy of the calling you have received" (Eph. 4:1).

It is again important to note that the word *urge* in this verse is translated from the same basic word *parakaleō* translated "to encourage" in other places in the New Testament. It is the same word Paul used in Romans 12:1. I personally believe it has the same basic meaning as that used by Luke as he described Barnabas' ministry in Antioch. Like Barnabas, Paul was about to "urge" or "encourage" the Christians in Ephesus to "remain true to the Lord with all their hearts." This is certainly what it means "to live a life *worthy* of the calling" we have received from Christ.

What we read in the second part of the Ephesian letter is in many aspects a parallel passage with Romans 12:1-2. However, as stated earlier, Paul is more descriptive in explaining what it means to actually live for Christ.

The parallel aspects between the Roman and Ephesian letters can be seen clearly in the following comparative study.

THE ROMAN LETTER God's Mercies (Chaps. 1—11)	THE EPHESIAN LETTER A Christian's Calling in Christ (Chaps. 1—3)
Therefore, I *urge* you, brothers, in view of God's mercy (Rom. 12:1).	As a prisoner for the Lord, then, I *urge* you to live a life worthy of the calling you have received (Eph. 4:1).

Therefore, I urge you . . . to *offer your bodies* as living sacrifices, holy and pleasing to God—which is your spiritual worship (v. 1).

So I tell you this, and insist on it in the Lord, that you must no longer live as the Gentiles do, in the *futility of their thinking.* They are *darkened in their understanding* and separated from the life of God because of the ignorance that is in them due to the *hardening of their hearts.* Having lost all sensitivity, they have given themselves over to sensuality so as *to indulge in every kind of impurity,* with a continual lust for more (vv. 17-19).

Do not conform any longer to the *pattern of this world* (v. 2).

You, however, did not come to know Christ that way. Surely you heard of Him and were *taught* of Him in accordance with the truth that is in Jesus. You were *taught,* with regard to your *former way of life,* to *put off your old self,* which is being corrupted by its deceitful desires (vv. 20-22).

But among you there must not be even a hint of *sexual immorality,* or of any kind of *impurity,* or of *greed,* because these are improper for God's holy people. Nor should there be *obscenity, foolish talk,* or *coarse joking,* which are out of place, but rather thanksgiving (5:3-4).

But be transformed by the *renewing of your mind* (v. 2).	You were taught . . . *to be made new in the attitude of your minds;* and to put on the new self, created to be like God in true righteousness and holiness (4:22-24).
Then you will be able to test and approve *what God's will is*—His good, pleasing, and perfect will (v. 2).	Be very careful, then, how you live—not as unwise, but as wise, making the most of every opportunity, because the days are evil. Therefore, do not be foolish, but *understand what the Lord's will is* (5:15-17).

One great need for New Testament Christians, especially those who were converted out of a pagan lifestyle, was to develop a *Christian* lifestyle that reflected God's holiness—particularly in the area of moral purity. The first-century world was definitely X-rated and Christians needed continual encouragement to "put off the old lifestyle" and to "put on the new lifestyle"—a lifestyle that reflected Jesus Christ Himself.

The 20th-Century Christian and the X-Rated World

There is a striking parallel between the first century and our own, with this exception. When Christianity was born, the entire world was basically immoral. A positive influence still remained from those few Jews who were attempting to obey God's laws. However, many of God's chosen people had been absorbed into the world's system. They had designed their own subtle style of immorality, based on theological rationalizations.

On the other hand, the American culture was brought into being by people who were at least outwardly committed to the values of Christianity. Originally they wrote these values into our society's laws. Though immorality has always existed, in recent years our sexual morality has rapidly declined. More and more, our whole society is moving toward open and flagrant immorality.

The Visual Media

Do books, movies, and television *reflect* or *cause* what is happening in our society? The answer, I believe, is both! Today—just as in Antioch, Rome, and Ephesus—the entertainment world both reflects and contributes to the moral decay that is taking place in our society.

There is hardly a current movie or television program that does not focus on immoral sex as a source of humor. One evening my wife and son and I decided to spend some time watching television. We literally switched from channel to channel and program to program—and everywhere we turned the subject was sex. The same trend, of course, is true in the theaters—only far worse.

Music

Secular music also reflects the morals of the day. Many popular songs flagrantly focus on fornication and adulterous relationships. Some songs are more philosophical. *My Way* reflects unadulterated selfishness. *I've Got to Be Me* also promotes a self-centered outlook. In other words, it really doesn't matter what you want—I come first—*my* needs, *my* interests, *my* concerns.

A friend and I went to see a man who had left his wife and family for another woman. Our hope was that we might convince him to return to his family—to come to his senses. His children were brokenhearted and disillusioned; his wife was desperately hurt and devastated. We found him in his apartment, where he again and again played the song, *I've Got to Be Me.* Trying to reason with him got us nowhere.

Illegitimate sex—premarital, marital infidelity, and homosexuality—are no longer activities that are read about and viewed in secret. They have come out of the closet. They surround us and permeate our culture.

What is a Christian to do? We must not, we dare not, allow ourselves to conform to the world's system. We must present our bodies to God—to honor Him. And we must renew our minds daily.

Our eyes and ears are the windows to our souls. There's no way we can feed our inner beings on things that are opposed to God's will without being affected by them spiritually and morally.

Observation Versus Participation

A strange philosophy is spreading today. Those who hold to this philosophy claim that to view other's sinning is not indulging in sin itself. Some Christians who never allow themselves to engage in illicit sexual activities either before or after marriage do not hesitate to enjoy the illicit experiences of others via literature, movies, or music.

How does God view this kind of behavior? Scripture shows that to indulge in the sexual exploits of others vicariously, and to laugh at vulgar jokes, border on the acts themselves. Remember Paul's exhortation to the Ephesians? "But among you," he wrote, "there must not be even a hint of sexual immorality, or any kind of impurity, or of greed, because these are improper for God's holy people. Nor should there be obscenity, foolish talk, or coarse joking, which are out of place, but rather thanksgiving" (Eph. 5:3-4).

Our Example as Parents

Most Christian parents are concerned about the moral values of their children. But many Christian parents don't realize that what they allow themselves to hear and see affects their children's moral values. What we *are* speaks so loudly that our children cannot hear what we *say*.

Even secular psychologists recognize the power of modeling values for our children. J. A. Hadfield, a British psychologist who observed the growth patterns of thousands of children, made the following observation: "We see that it is by a perfectly natural process that the child develops standards of behavior and a moral sense. So that if you never taught a child one single moral maxim, he would nevertheless develop moral—or immoral—standards of right and wrong by the process of identification" *(Childhood and Adolescence,* Penguin Books, p. 134).

Peer Pressure

An unfortunate phenomenon is taking place in our culture, particularly among young people. It's called "peer pressure." It can best be illustrated by this article taken from a 1980 issue of *The Dallas Morning News,* entitled "Virginity Loses to Peer Pressure."

In less than a generation, the number of teenagers who have had sexual intercourse by age 16 has increased eight-fold as "sexually obligated" youths face strong peer pressure to lose their virginity, *Ladies Home Journal* said.

"The pressure is based on a sense (sometimes inaccurate) that everybody's doing it and that anyone who's a virgin is out of step with the times," the *Journal* said in the March issue. It said the pressure is applied to both boys and girls.

The magazine quoted several experts as saying 16 is the youngest most people can experience sex without suffering psychological problems.

One 16-year-old girl told the magazine:

"I'm a virgin. Isn't it pathetic? I don't think any of my friends are. They don't criticize me, but it's like a barrier between them and me. Like they know something I don't. It makes me feel left out. I'm definitely going to do it before my 17th birthday. I don't know with who. I'm looking forward to being able to tell my friends, 'Guess what? Look what I did.'"

There's also peer pressure among adults in taking a stand for moral issues—even in relatively simple decisions. I remember watching a television program one evening with a group of Christian friends. As the program progressed, it became clear that the subject matter was becoming increasingly immoral. All of us were getting a bit nervous and finally one person got up enough courage to change the channel. When that happened, everyone breathed a sigh of relief. I remember I felt pressure *not* to be the one to make the decision, lest I be considered "square" or "old fashioned." I think everyone else felt the same pressure. What a satanic trick!

Today, more than at any time in the history of our culture, Christians must *encourage one another* to remain true to the Lord with all their hearts (Acts 11:23). And the most basic meaning of this kind of encouragement involves maintaining moral purity in all of our behavior and relationships.

Life Response

Christians must do at least two things to properly use our eyes and ears in order to renew our minds.

1. *We must concentrate on "excellent" and "praiseworthy" things as revealed in the Word of God.* "Finally, brothers, whatever is true, whatever is noble, whatever is right, whatever is pure, whatever is lovely, whatever is admirable— if anything is excellent or praiseworthy—think about such things" (Phil. 4:8).

   To what extent do you renew your mind with Scripture and other good and noble thoughts?

2. *We must avoid concentrating on the things of the world.* "Do not love the world or anything in the world. If anyone loves the world, the love of the Father is not in him. For everything in the world—the cravings of sinful man, the lust of his eyes and the boasting of what he has and does—comes not from the Father, but from the world" (1 John 2:15-16).

   To what extent do we avoid concentrating on the things of this world that will hinder our Christian growth?

   A final question: *To what extent are we remaining true to the Lord with all our hearts?*

7

A Message of Encouragement

Under the leadership of Barnabas and Saul, the church at Antioch continued to grow and expand its influence. Little did either of these men realize what God had planned for them when they teamed up to pastor and teach these new Christians.

One day while they were "worshiping the Lord and fasting," along with several other key church leaders, the Holy Spirit spoke directly to them and said, "Set apart for me Barnabas and Saul for the work to which I have called them" (Acts 13:2).

God's revelation was clear! Their specific ministry in Antioch was finished. The Lord had another work outlined for them. Recognizing this to be true, the other men who shared in their "missionary call" continued to fast and pray with them, and eventually, Luke records that "they placed their hands on them and sent them off" (v. 3).

Under the direct leadership of the Holy Spirit, Barnabas and Saul traveled first to Seleucia and from there to Salamis and Paphos on the island of Cyprus. Eventually they continued on to Perga in Pamphylia. At this juncture John Mark left them and traveled back to Jerusalem, and Saul and Barnabas went on to Pisidian Antioch (vv. 4-12).

When Barnabas and Saul arrived in the city they entered the Jewish synagogue on the Sabbath Day, sat down, and listened to one of the Jewish rulers read from the Old Testament. The synagogue rulers recognized Barnabas and Saul as strangers, and as was customary they "sent word to them, saying, 'Brothers, if you have a *message of encouragement* for the people, please speak'" (v. 15).

Little did these men realize what they were asking, for this was the kind of opportunity Barnabas and Paul were looking for (from this point forward in Luke's narrative, Saul is called Paul). Paul immediately took the initiative, stood up, and spoke.

An important change takes place here. A year before, Barnabas had invited Paul to join him in Antioch to assist him in the ministry. Barnabas was the primary leader, for he was more mature in Christ. But now, in Pisidian Antioch, Paul began to emerge as the leader of the missionary team. In fact, from this point forward, Luke actually reverses the order of their names, mentioning Paul first in the historical record. (See Acts 13:42-43, 46, 50; 14:1, 3, 23; 15:2, 12, 22, 35.)

Again this speaks volumes regarding Barnabas' character. He recognized in his friend even greater abilities than in himself and quickly acknowledged God's special apostolic calling in Paul's life. Without hesitation, he encouraged Paul to take the primary leadership role. Here in Pisidian Antioch, we see Barnabas, Son of Encouragement, listening to his friend Paul deliver a profound and exciting "message of encouragement" of his own—a message Barnabas probably had in essence given many times. Other than the example of Jesus Christ, this is probably the most graphic illustration of discipling methodology in the whole New Testament.

Paul's Message of Encouragement (Acts 13:16-41)

Addressing both Jews and God-fearing Gentiles, Paul first succinctly summarized God's dealings with Israel, how He:
- "Chose our fathers" (Acts 13:17)
- "Made the people prosper during their stay in Egypt" (v. 17)
- "Led them out of that country" (v. 17)
- "Endured their conduct 40 years in the desert" (v. 18)
- "Overthrew seven nations in Canaan" (v. 19)
- "Gave their land to His people (v. 19)
- "Gave them judges" (v. 20)
- "Gave them Saul [to be their king]" (v. 21)
- "Made David their king" (v. 22)

All of this, Paul implied, set the stage for the greatest event of all. From David's descendants "God has brought to Israel the

Saviour Jesus, as He promised" (v. 23). But, continued Paul, as Jews we "did not recognize Jesus" and had Him condemned to death in spite of the fact that there was "no proper ground for a death sentence" (vv. 27-28).

Toward the end of his message Paul focused on the Resurrection and what that means to *both* Jews and Gentiles. Four times he emphasized that the grave could not hold Jesus Christ:

- But *God raised Him from the dead,* and for many days he was seen by those who had traveled with Him from Galilee to Jerusalem. They are now His witnesses to our people (vv. 30-31).

- We tell you the Good News: What God promised our fathers He has fulfilled for us, their children, by *raising up Jesus* (vv. 32-33).

- The fact that *God raised Him from the dead,* never to decay, is stated in these words: "I will give you the holy and sure blessings promised to David" (v. 34).

- For when David had served God's purpose in his own generation, he fell asleep; he was buried with his fathers and his body decayed. But the One whom *God raised from the dead* did not see decay (vv. 36-37).

Paul's culminating statement in this message is one of the most *encouraging* "therefore" statements in all of Scripture:

Therefore, my brothers, I want you to know that through Jesus the *forgiveness of sins* is proclaimed to you. Through Him *everyone who believes is justified from everything* you could not be justified from by the law of Moses (vv. 38-39).

All of Christian history rests on this one fact—the resurrection of Jesus Christ. As Paul wrote to the Corinthians, "If Christ has not been raised, our preaching is useless and so is your faith," but continued Paul, "Christ *has* indeed been raised from the dead" (1 Cor. 15:14, 20). This was the essence of Paul's *message of encouragement* in Pisidian Antioch.

Paul and the Resurrection

Many evidences demonstrate that the resurrection of Christ is a fact of history. But perhaps none is so outstanding as what actually happened to Paul. His message in Pisidian Antioch leaves no doubt that he believed that the physical resurrection of Jesus Christ was indeed a *fact* of history. References to this event permeate the letters he wrote. Why was he so sure when at one time he actually denied the resurrection of Christ so vehemently that he imprisoned people who believed it and even consented to their death? We can only answer that question when we have a larger perspective.

The Historical Setting

Think for a moment what had happened after Christ was crucified. His body was removed from the cross and placed in a cave-like tomb. A stone so large that it took several people to move it covered the entrance. Since Christ had stated repeatedly that He would rise from the dead on the third day, the Jewish leaders had stationed guards by the tomb. The leaders were afraid that Jesus' disciples would try to steal His body and then propagate a lie that He had in fact risen (Matt. 27:62-64).

The disciples were filled with fear. They were totally demoralized. Their faith was almost nonexistent and their memories blurred. Intellectually and emotionally, they were not convinced that Christ would rise again.

Under these conditions, it was inconceivable that they would attempt to steal the body, and even more inconceivable that they would start a rumor. From their viewpoint there was no reason to do so. They would reap no positive benefits. Rather, they would actually be taking their lives in their own hands. Should they be caught, they might also be condemned to death.

The disciples did not believe Christ was going to rise again. This attitude is illustrated by the women who came to the tomb on Sunday morning. They came to anoint Christ's body—totally expecting that His body would be there. In fact, they concluded that the Lord's body had been stolen by His enemies (John 20:2, 13). When Peter and John found out that the body was missing and they ran to the empty tomb, they also did not believe that Christ had risen (vv. 3-5). In fact, "they still did not understand from Scripture that Jesus had to rise from the dead" (v. 9).

The guards and the Jewish rulers knew more than the disciples. Matthew reports that the guards felt an earthquake and saw an angel of the Lord come down from heaven and move the stone away from the entrance of Christ's tomb. These men "were so afraid . . . that they shook and became like dead men" (Matt. 28:4). But once they regained their equilibrium, some of them rushed into the city and "reported to the chief priests everything that had happened" (v. 11).

Obviously, something supernatural had happened to Christ's body. To hide this fact, the religious leaders were forced to do the same thing they were afraid the disciples of Jesus would do. They planned and propagated a lie. Their lie of course was *not* that Christ had risen, but that "His disciples came during the night and stole Him away" while the guards were asleep (v. 13).

So there were the Jewish leaders—knowing that Christ's body had disappeared supernaturally but telling people that His disciples had stolen the body. And there were the disciples, knowing *nothing* of those supernatural events and thinking that their enemies had removed His body.

The disciples believed only after they saw Jesus alive. It took far more than an empty tomb to convince them that Christ was risen. It was only when they actually saw Him alive—saw the nailprints in His hands and the spear wound in His side—that they believed He had indeed risen from the grave (John 20:19-20).

During the next 40 days Christ appeared numerous times to many people. As Luke reports, He "gave *many convincing proofs* that He was alive" (Acts 1:3). Then His 11 disciples, on a mountaintop in Galilee, heard Jesus speak with them face to face for the last time, and finally saw Him ascend to heaven.

Then they returned to Jerusalem and waited for the promised Holy Spirit. On the Day of Pentecost the Holy Spirit came! Suddenly a timid and fearful group of people became a mighty force in Jerusalem. No longer were they confused and disillusioned about who Jesus was and what had happened to Him. Again and again they proclaimed the news that Jesus had risen. In fact, every recorded sermon Peter preached in the early days focused on the Resurrection (2:24, 32; 3:15; 4:2, 10; 5:30).

The Jewish leaders seemingly made no attempt to prove that the

Resurrection was a hoax. Though the religious leaders were quite disturbed with the growing belief in the Resurrection, they evidently did very little to actually *prove* that Jesus had not miraculously disappeared. Had His body been stolen, they would have done everything possible to produce the corpse and once and for all prove the Resurrection story was a myth. This would have been the logical way to destroy the Christian movement, for without the Resurrection it would have died a natural death.

But this was not their approach. Why not? First, the chief priests and elders of Israel *knew* something miraculous had happened because of the report from the guards. Secondly, and perhaps most importantly, the body was no longer in Joseph's grave. Even if the religious leaders had tried to find the body, which it appears they did not, it was nowhere to be found.

It is incongruous to believe that the disciples would literally give their lives to propagate a myth. If the disciples had stolen the body, and then proclaimed Christ had risen—while they had hidden the corpse in some other place—how do we explain why a fearful and confused and doubting group of people would devise a myth and become willing to suffer persecution and die for something that was not true? Every ounce of reason and every thread of logic points unwaveringly to the fact that this could never happen. It is too preposterous.

The fact is that there was no body in the grave! The disciples of Jesus knew this beyond a shadow of doubt because they had walked and talked with the risen Christ. They had seen Him once again work miracles. They *knew* who He was. On the other hand, the Jewish leaders knew the body had miraculously disappeared—but they were unwilling to admit to the Resurrection, and they were totally unable to disprove it. All they could do was to irrationally *deny it*—and to try to squelch a body of people who knew from direct experience that Christ had risen. But it didn't work!

Saul (Paul) Enters the Scene

During the rapid growth of the church, Saul emerged as a dominant personality in Jerusalem. He was a devout Jew—a Hebrew of the Hebrews and a Pharisee. He had studied under Gamaliel, one of the finest Jewish teachers of his day (Acts 22:3).

There's some difference of opinion as to Saul's whereabouts during the crucifixion and the early days of the church. Was he absent from Jerusalem? If so, when did he arrive back on the scene? Did he passively observe the events surrounding Christ's trial and crucifixion, and then suddenly step forward to become an overt enemy of Christianity? Or did he come back to Jerusalem at the height of the controversy regarding the Resurrection and then become immediately involved? We do not know the answers to these questions. But when Saul appeared on the scene, he immediately took matters into his own hands and began a countermovement to wipe out Christianity.

Stephen was the first to die for his faith in the risen Christ. Luke's record is clear that "Saul was there, giving approval to his death" (8:1). This was just the beginning. Saul was relentless in his attacks on Christians, and soon extended his efforts to stamp out Christianity beyond Jerusalem.

But while on the road to Damascus with permission from the high priest to search out Christians and bring them back as prisoners to Jerusalem, something dramatic happened. He became a changed man. He became a Christian himself and quickly began to proclaim the same message he denied and for which he had put people to death.

How do we explain such extreme behavior? Why would a brilliant man like Saul suddenly join his enemies? Why would he totally reverse his thinking? What would cause a man of his prominence to withdraw into quiet isolation in Arabia, spend at least nine patient years in Tarsus, and then suffer all of the different and trying persecutions over the years as he preached the message he once denied? What would cause him to in the end give his own life in martyrdom for the cause of Christianity?

It must be said first of all that Paul did not go berserk! There's absolutely no evidence of any mental or emotional breakdown. Neither did he have an emotional experience that turned him into a hysterical person. Paul's brilliant mind was intact till the end of his life. This is evident from his letters, which represent some of the most logical and scholarly material written in the first century. An insane or emotionally disturbed man could never have accomplished what Paul accomplished in Christian history!

Only one logical answer explains why Saul changed so dramatically. He discovered he was mistaken. He discovered that Christ *is* the Messiah. He discovered that Christ *was* crucified and on the third day He *arose again*. Paul had a visual encounter with the risen Christ. He was converted. What happened to him had happened to hundreds before him—men such as Peter and John and the other apostles. When Saul encountered Jesus Christ on the road to Damascus, the logic of it all fell in place. As Frank Morison states:

> When Saul was really convinced that he had seen the risen Jesus, the immense and overpowering significance of the empty tomb swept for the first time into his mind. It was as though the great stone itself had crashed into and carried away his last defenses. He saw that if the disciples were not deceivers, then they were *right*—right through the whole range and gamut of their claim. He realized why one could not associate a martyrdom so glorious as that of Stephen with a vulgar deception involving connivance with the abduction of a corpse. He began to understand why Peter was so sure and why everyone connected with the movement was so unaccountably joyous and so immovably convinced.
>
> And the curious thing is—indeed, it is the master circumstance of all this strange story—that once this conviction had been reached, its effect on any normally constituted mind was enduring. The vacancy of the tomb was a historic fact—fixed and unalterable. Its authority grew rather than declined with the passing of the years. It was never shaken throughout Paul's lifetime, and in the writer's judgment it remains unshaken to this day (*Who Moved the Stone?* Zondervan, p. 145).

A 20th-Century Witness

As a young man and a member of the Church of England, Frank Morison would struggle during the reading of the Apostles' Creed. He participated to a point, but once he reached the statement that Jesus Christ "suffered under Pontius Pilate, was crucified, dead, and buried," he would at this point "stop dead" and "set his teeth tightly" and "refuse to utter another word." He believed that Jesus Christ lived and died, but he did *not* believe in the Resurrection (*Who Moved the Stone?* p. 67).

Consequently, Mr. Morison set out to prove that the Resurrection was a hoax. Using all the historical documents he could find, he carefully and methodically studied the events surrounding

Christ's crucifixion. In addition to the New Testament, he studied the writings of Josephus, the great Jewish historian, and the extra-biblical documents such as the Gospel of Peter, the Gospel of Nicodemus, and the Gospel to the Hebrews.

Finally he *did* write a book. But the first chapter was titled "The Book that Refused to be Written." In some respects, like Paul, he was dramatically changed. He had no vision, and heard no voice. But during his objective study of history, Frank Morison proved to himself that Christ had indeed risen from the dead.

At one point in Mr. Morison's reporting of his findings regarding the Resurrection, he stated:

> I have wrestled with that problem and found it tougher than ever I could have conceived possible. It is easy to say that you will believe nothing that will not fit into the mold of a rationalist's conception of the universe. But suppose the facts won't fit into that mold? The utmost that an honest man can do is to undertake to examine the facts patiently and impartially, and to see where they lead him *(Who Moved the Stone?* p. 67).

Both Christian and religious history itself bear witness to this fact. G.B. Hardy summarized it well when he wrote: "Here is the complete record:

> Confucius' tomb—occupied
> Buddha's tomb—occupied
> Mohammed's tomb—occupied
> Jesus' tomb—EMPTY."

(Taken from Josh McDowell's book, *Evidence That Demands a Verdict,* Campus Crusade for Christ, p. 270.)

In the words of Josh McDowell, "The decision is now yours to make; the evidence speaks for itself. It says very clearly, Christ is risen indeed" *(Evidence That Demands,* p. 270).

In essence this was Paul's message of encouragement that day in Pisidia in Antioch. And there were those who wanted to hear more. They invited Paul and Barnabas "to speak further about these things on the next Sabbath" (Acts 13:42).

Hopefully, this is also your attitude regarding Paul's *message of encouragement.* You want to know more too! If you are not a Christian, consider carefully Paul's powerful *therefore* statement in the closing portion of his message. "Therefore, my brothers, I want you to know that through Jesus the *forgiveness of sins* is proclaimed to you. Through Him everyone *who believes is justified from everything* you could not be justified from by the Law of Moses" (vv. 38-39).

Have you received Christ's forgiveness? Do you really *believe* He died for you? You can do that now—as Paul himself did that day on the road to Damascus. You need not *see* the living Christ to believe. In fact, Jesus said to doubting Thomas, "Because you have seen Me, you have believed; *blessed are those who have not seen and yet have believed*" (John 20:29).

A Prayer of Invitation

Father, I _____ believe that Jesus
died for my sins and rose again on the third day. And
_(name) because He lives, I believe I will live also—eternally. Thank You for entering my life and making me a Christian.

8

Living for Christ in an Unbelieving World

Paul and Barnabas launched their first missionary journey from Antioch in Syria. There they had spent a year together as a team involved in intensive evangelism, as well as encouraging and teaching new believers (Acts 11:25-26). It was there they received a very direct and specific call from the Holy Spirit to travel west (13:2), first to Cyprus and then on to Perga in Pamphylia (see map).

At this point they headed north and soon arrived in Pisidian Antioch. They entered the Jewish synagogue and Paul delivered his stirring "message of encouragement" with a focus on the resurrection of Jesus Christ (v. 15ff). A number of people responded to the Gospel. In fact, interest was so great that it created jealousy among the key Jewish leaders in the city. Consequently they "stirred up persecution against Paul and Barnabas, and expelled them from this region" (v. 50).

Undaunted, Paul and Barnabas traveled on to Iconium (v. 51) and eventually to Lystra and Derbe (14:8, 20). Though persecution followed them from city to city, so did God's blessing on their ministry. People everywhere responded to their message and became followers of Jesus Christ.

In spite of the hostility that was generated in the various cities because of their evangelistic success, Paul and Barnabas decided to retrace their steps and spend some time with these new Christians. Consequently they "returned to Lystra, Iconium, and Antioch,

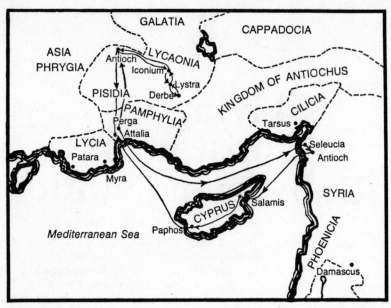

strengthening the disciples and encouraging them to remain true to the faith" (vv. 21-22).

In many respects this statement made by Luke in Acts 14:21-22 parallels rather closely another statement which he recorded regarding Barnabas' ministry in Antioch and Syria, which is illustrated as follows:

Acts 11:23	Acts 14:21-22
When he [Barnabas] arrived [in Antioch Syria] and saw the evidence of the grace of God, he was glad and . . .	Then they returned to Lystra, Iconium, and Antioch, strengthening the disciples and . . .
encouraged them all to remain true to the Lord with all their hearts.	*encouraging them to remain true to the faith.*

The parallelism in these two statements shows that the emphasis of each ministry was one of *encouragement.* It is also clear from the fact that these new believers were encouraged "to *remain true."* There seems to be variance because the Christians in the first location were encouraged to *"remain true to the Lord,"* and in the second location they were encouraged "to remain true *to the faith."*

Is this really a variance in meaning? Doesn't "to remain *true to the Lord"* mean the same thing as "to remain *true to the faith"?* The answer must be yes if we understand that to "remain true to the Lord" is a comprehensive statement including not only *what* we believe but *how* we live. The answer is no (that is, there *is* a variance in meaning) when we understand that to "remain true *to the faith"* puts an emphasis on that aspect of Christian growth that relates more specifically to *what* we believe.

This can be explained with two circles (see diagram). "To remain *true to the Lord"* is represented by the larger circle. "To remain true *to the faith"* is represented by the smaller circle. However, the smaller circle is an integral part of the larger circle. This means that "to remain true *to the faith"* is central and foundational to Christianity, but is only a part of the larger concept—"to remain true *to the Lord."*

This variance can also be illustrated by several of the New

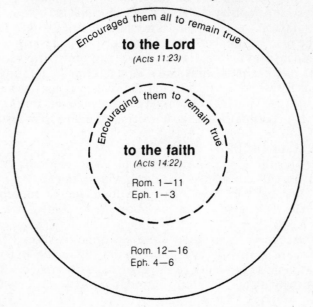

Encouraged them all to remain true

to the Lord
(Acts 11:23)

Encouraging them to remain true

to the faith
(Acts 14:22)

Rom. 1—11
Eph. 1—3

Rom. 12—16
Eph. 4—6

Testament letters. If we read Romans, chapters 1—11, or Ephesians chapters 1—3, we see that Paul is emphasizing *what* we believe. He is encouraging Christians to "remain true to the faith." However, when we read Romans 12—16 or Ephesians 4—6, Paul is emphasizing *how to live* in the light of *what* a Christian should believe. He encourages believers not only "to remain ture *to the faith*" but also, in the total sense, to "remain true *to the Lord.*"

So when Barnabas encouraged the believers in Antioch in Syria to "remain true to the Lord," he was emphasizing both the *what* and *how* of Christianity—but perhaps with a *special* emphasis on the *how*. This seems to be true from the context. Barnabas was concerned that these new believers not continue to conform their lives to the world but to be transformed into the image of Christ (Rom. 12:1-2). That is also why these disciples of Christ in Antioch were eventually called *Christians*. They were indeed reflecting Christ's life in their lives.

However, when Paul and Barnabas returned to Lystra, Iconium, and Antioch, encouraging the believers "to remain true to the faith," they concentrated on the *what* of Christianity. Obviously their teaching ministry did not exclude an emphasis on *how* to live, for it is difficult to imagine them teaching doctrine without dealing with the practical implications of that doctrine in a Christian's life. But it does seem that their *emphasis* on this return trip was on the basic faith-content of Christianity. And this should not surprise us, particularly when we understand the dynamics that were taking place in those cities. Let's look at those dynamics. But first, let's clarify the concept of faith as it is depicted in the New Testament.

Three Concepts of Faith

There are three major concepts of faith used in the New Testament. All are related, yet distinct in meaning.

The first is *saving faith*. This is a foundational concept. The Bible clearly teaches that salvation is by faith, not works (Eph. 2:8-9).

The second is *living faith*. Once we come to know Christ *by faith,* we are to also *live* by faith, reflecting this quality in our lives. In fact, doing so is a mark of Christian maturity among believers. This is why Paul frequently introduced his letters to various churches by thanking God for *their faith* (Eph. 1:15; Col. 1:4; 1 Thes. 1:3; 2 Thes. 1:3).

The third concept of faith is that referred to in Acts 14: 22—when Paul and Barnabas decided to return to Lystra, Iconium, and Antioch to encourage these Christians *"to remain true to the faith."* Here the word faith refers to a system of beliefs, a body of truth and doctrine. It involves the basic content of Christianity. It was because of *what* these Christians believed that they were being persecuted. And it was the burden of Paul and Barnabas to strengthen and encourage those new believers to continue in *the faith* they had been taught. Let's look now more specifically at *why* this kind of emphasis was necessary.

These Christians were being persecuted because of what they believed. Precipitated primarily by jealousy among the unbelieving Jews, who denied that Jesus was the Christ, intense persecution broke out in the three cities mentioned in Acts 14:21 (Lystra, Iconium, and Antioch). In Antioch the interest in what Paul and Barnabas were teaching was so high that "almost the whole city gathered to hear the Word of the Lord." But "when the Jews saw the crowds, they were filled with jealousy and talked abusively against what Paul was saying" (13:44-45). Eventually, "they stirred up persecution against Paul and Barnabas, and expelled them from their region" (v. 50).

These two missionaries then traveled on to Iconium, and again the Lord granted them unusual success. Luke records that "There they spoke so effectively that a great number of Jews and Gentiles believed" (14:1). But again, persecution! "The Jews who *refused to believe* stirred up the Gentiles and poisoned their minds against the brothers" (v. 2) and eventually they had to leave Iconium because of a plot to take their lives.

The next stop was Lystra, where Paul healed a man who was lame from birth. The impact was so great on the Lycaonian people that they thought their gods had come down to them in human form. Overwhelmed with awe, they tried to worship Paul and Barnabas. This strange turn of events gave these two missionaries opportunity to explain the Good News regarding the one true God who had indeed appeared in human form, the form of Jesus Christ.

In the meantime, a number of Jews from Antioch and Iconium followed Paul and Barnabas to Lystra. When they arrived, they succeeded in turning the people against Paul and Barnabas. In this instance, they actually succeeded in having Paul stoned. In fact, so successful was their attempt on his life that they thought he was dead and dragged him outside the city.

But then came the greatest miracle of all. While Paul lay there, a number of disciples gathered around him. Suddenly he stood up and on his own walked back into the city. Some commentators believe Paul was actually killed, and that God raised him from the dead. In any case, God healed Paul, and used this event to confirm the truth of the message Paul and Barnabas were preaching.

Their next stop was Derbe, where again response to the Gospel was enormous (v. 21). It was in this city that Paul and Barnabas made the decision to retrace their steps and return to Lystra, Iconium, and Antioch to *encourage* the new Christian converts "to remain true to the faith" (v. 22). As we look at the larger context in which all of this was taking place, we can see why they made this decision. These new Christians were living in the midst of unbelievers who were intent on stamping out Christianity through persecution. Obviously, the attacks did not stop when Paul and Barnabas were eventually driven out of each city. The persecution went on, and Paul and Barnabas were deeply concerned that these new Christians "remain true to *the faith*" in the midst of the attacks.

Another New Testament Illustration
Persecution against Christians by unbelievers continued to be a New Testament phenomenon. Sometime later Paul and another missionary companion named Silas and also a young man named Timothy were making a second missionary journey. Their travels took them to Thessalonica, where they immediately began to share the Good News of Christ. After a period of time a number of people, both Jews and Gentiles, responded to the Gospel (17:4).

By now the Jewish reaction was predictable. Luke records that they "were jealous" and "rounded up some bad characters from the marketplace, formed a mob, and started a riot in the city" (v. 5). Pressure got so great that Paul and Silas had to leave the city by night in order to escape harm (v. 10).

Once Paul and his co-workers were forced to leave Thessalonica, their concerns were the same as they had been on earlier occasions. What would happen to these new believers? Would they give in to the continuing persecution and turn from their faith?

In this instance, it was not possible for Paul and Silas to return to Thessalonica, even though they desperately wanted to. However, they were able to send Timothy, and Paul shared a detailed account of this concern in a letter he later wrote and sent to this church. "When we could stand it no longer," he wrote, "we thought it best to be left by ourselves in Athens. We sent Timothy, who is our brother and God's fellow worker in spreading the Gospel of Christ, to *strengthen* and *encourage you in your faith.*" Then Paul stated why they were so concerned—"so that no one would be unsettled by these trials" (1 Thes. 3:1-3).

Four more times in this brief passage Paul referred to his concern about their *faith:*

> For this reason, [because of persecution] when I could stand it no longer, I sent to find out about *your faith* (3:5).

> Timothy has just now come to us from you and has brought good news about *your faith* (v. 6).

> Therefore, brothers, in all our distress and persecution we were *encouraged* about you because of *your faith* (v. 7). (Here Paul demonstrates that encouragement is a mutual and reciprocal process.)

> Night and day we pray most earnestly that we may see you again and supply what is lacking in *your faith* (v. 10).

Remaining True to the Faith Today

One of Satan's greatest tactics is to confuse Christians regarding what they should believe. The 20th century, as perhaps no other time in history, is filled with many voices "crying in the wilderness." Unfortunately, many of these voices claim to be presenting the true message of God.

One evening I was driving from the Dallas/Fort Worth Airport to my home. I turned on the radio and just happened to tune in on an open-line talk show, originating in California. The man behind the microphone was receiving calls from the listening audience and dialoguing about Christianity. It didn't take long to detect that this man—as intelligent and fluent as he was—was not representing *the* faith as it is taught in Scripture. The first clue came when someone asked him if he believed that Jesus Christ was one with God. Though he acknowledged that Jesus was a great teacher and even the Son of God, he explained that Jesus was *not* one with God—that He could not be, and gave various reasons. I believe I'm fair when I say that not one of his reasons was based in Scripture.

The more I listened to this man, the more I could detect that his view of Jesus Christ was not the only error in his theology. I was amazed at how many people accepted what he was saying as representing what the Bible really taught.

The Doctrine of Christ

As you study the world's major religions as well as the various offshoots of Christianity, you discover they all agree on one major issue—that Jesus Christ was not *one* with God. Though most of these religious groups concede that He was a great teacher and some even call Him the Son of God, they deny His divine nature as it is defined in Scripture. Many, of course, also deny that He was physically raised from the dead.

This was a major point of contention with the message Paul and Barnabas were teaching on their first missionary journey. Their view of Christ departed radically from that of their Jewish brothers in the flesh. This led to a great deal of disagreement and eventually persecution.

What does the Bible teach about Jesus Christ? Though we do not have time to develop this truth in depth, the following statements and Scripture references represent what Christians have believed about Jesus Christ since the first century (and appears in our own doctrinal statement at Fellowship Bible Church):

> We believe that God the Son became flesh in Jesus Christ, who was conceived by the Holy Spirit and born of the virgin Mary, and who is both God and man (John 1:14; Matt. 1:18-25; 27:54; John 11:33; 8:4; Heb. 1:8; 2:14).

We also believe in the bodily resurrection of Christ, and His ascension into heaven, and in His present life there for us. Jesus now serves as High Priest, Intercessor, and Advocate on our behalf with the Father (Rom. 1:4; John 20:25-27; 1 John 2:1; Heb. 7:25; Mark 16:19; Acts 1:9-11).

The Doctrine of Salvation

Closely aligned with the doctrine of Christ is a Christian's view of salvation. Religions that depart from what the Bible teaches in this area believe that people are saved by works. Many believe that man is basically good and can earn his way to heaven. Others believe that all will be saved (the doctrine of universalism). Many teach that there are "many ways" to heaven. They all believe, however, that their way is the *best* way.

I remember talking to a young lady in the Boston airport one day. She represented the Hare Krishna religion, which has its roots in oriental mysticism. As we talked I explained I was a Christian—a follower of Jesus Christ.

"Oh, that's OK," she said. "You follow Jesus and we follow our religious leader. But we're all heading in the same direction."

"But you don't understand," I responded. "I believe Jesus Christ is the *only* way to heaven." Then I quoted what He said to His disciples in the Upper Room: "I am the way—and the truth and the life. No one comes to the Father except through Me" (John 14:6).

"Oh, that's OK, too," she responded. "That's what *He* believed. There are other men who taught that there were other ways. But they were all teaching the same thing."

At that point, of course, there wasn't much I could say. The fact is that Jesus Christ *did* teach that He was the only way to heaven. There is no other way to interpret the Bible. And, if God is who He says He is, and if Jesus is who He says He is, there is no other interpretation that makes sense.

The Bible teaches that we cannot work our way to heaven. It is only by faith in Christ. This was why Jesus said earlier to Nicodemus, "Whoever believes in the Son has eternal life, but whoever rejects the Son will not see life, for God's wrath remains on him" (3:36).

Again, many statements in Scripture verify that salvation is by faith in Jesus Christ. However, the following statements help summarize what the Bible actually teaches:

> We believe that the first man and woman were created in the image of God and thus, man has great value in God's sight. But man sinned and consequently experienced not only physical death, but also spiritual death (which is separation from God). The consequences of this sin affect the entire human race. All human beings are born with a sinful nature and, in the case of those who reach moral responsibility, commit acts of sin (Gen. 1:26-27; 2:17; 3:6; Rom. 5:12-19; Eph. 2:1-3, 4:18; Mark 7:20-23; John 2:24-25).

> We believe that Jesus Christ died for the sins of all humanity as a substitutionary sacrifice and that all who believe in Him are declared righteous on the basis of His shed blood (2 Cor. 5:14; Mark 10:45; Rom. 3:24-26, 5:8-9; 1 Pet. 3:18).

> We believe that whoever by faith receives Jesus Christ as his Saviour becomes a child of God. This salvation is not the result of any human effort or merit (John 1:12; Eph. 2:8-9; Rom. 3:28).

> We believe in the bodily resurrection of all men. Believers are resurrected to enjoy eternal life with God. Unbelievers are resurrected to experience judgment and then eternal suffering apart from God (1 Cor. 15:52; 1 Thes. 4:6; Rev. 20:4-6, 12-15, 21:1-8; John 5:28-29; Dan. 12:2).

The Doctrine of the Trinity

Closely aligned with the false view of Christ as He relates to God is the doctrine of the Trinity. The majority of cults and isms that are offshoots of Christianity deny the doctrine of the Trinity. Though it is true that the writers of Scripture never use the word *Trinity,* the truth is clearly derived from what the New Testament

Christians believed and taught. Therefore, we can make a statement as follows, which reflects what the Bible actually teaches:

We believe in one God eternally existing in three equal Persons—Father, Son, and Holy Spirit (John 14:9-10, 15:26; Heb. 1:8; Acts 5:3-4; Deut. 6:4; 2 Cor. 13:14; Matt. 28:19; Isa. 48:16).

Several months ago I received a call from a good friend who pastors a church in Illinois. One of the significant church leaders and his wife had been convinced by a local Bible teacher that the Bible does not teach the concept of the Trinity. My friend called seeking counsel as to what to do.

My pastor friend felt that the man and his wife were teachable and willing to study what the Bible had to say on the subject. So I directed him to Paul's instructions to Timothy: "Don't have anything to do with foolish and stupid arguments, because you know they produce quarrels. And the Lord's servant must not quarrel; instead, he must be kind to everyone, able to teach, not resentful. Those who oppose him you must gently instruct, in the hope that God will grant them repentance leading them to a knowledge of the truth, and that they will come to their senses and escape from the trap of the devil, who has taken them captive to do his will" (2 Tim. 2:23-26).

Consequently, the man and his wife and my friend agreed to spend two days together studying the Scriptures on the subject. They also agreed to invite a professor from a well-known Bible college to lead them in their study.

The results were exciting. Two days later, the man and his wife admitted they had been deceived, and later acknowledged it to the whole church. A careful study of the Bible led by gracious, knowledgeable people convinced them that they were wrong. Their change of viewpoint restored a beautiful unity among the leadership of the church, which affected the whole body of Christ.

The Doctrine of the Bible

In New Testament days the apostles themselves, who were directly taught by the Holy Spirit, were the primary source of authority in matters of truth. Much of what they taught was eventually written down and became part of the New Testament.

Many evidences show that the Bible as we have it today is indeed the authoritative Word of God. Therefore, we can state:

> We believe that the words of the Old and New Testaments are verbally inspired by God and are without error in the original manuscripts. The exact meaning of the Bible is essentially unchanged in any important respect in the widely accepted English translations. The Bible is authoritative and without error in any category of knowledge, including science and history, and is of supreme and final authority in all matters about which it speaks. We believe the Bible is to be interpreted in a normal and literal way and that it is understood as the believer is guided by the Spirit of God (John 10:35; Matt. 5:18; 2 Tim. 3:16; 2 Peter 1:21; 1 Tim. 5:18; 1 Cor. 2:13-16; John 16:12-15).

This is an important statement of doctrine, especially because today many well-meaning Christians are questioning whether or not the Bible is free from error. The fact is that if we cannot trust the Bible totally, there is no source of truth that we *can* trust. Once we open the door and teach that the Bible contains errors, it leads to other serious doctrinal problems.

Life Response
How well do you know the Bible? How well do you know *what* you believe—about the Bible, God, Jesus Christ, Christ's death, man and sin, the Holy Spirit, the church, angels, Satan, demons, salvation, and things to come? These are important Christian doctrines. In a world permeated with so much that is false and misleading, we need to continually *encourage one another* to learn more about Christian doctrines. If you have been a Christian for years and have studied the Bible little—following are several suggestions for increasing your knowledge of Christian doctrine:

1. Study a good book on doctrine, such as Paul Little's book, *Know What You Believe* (also published by Victor).

2. Attend a class on doctrine in your local church or in an evening Bible institute or college.

3. Develop your own personal and regular Bible study program.

A Challenge: Remember that you cannot encourage other Christians *with* sound doctrine unless you *know* sound doctrine.

9

Another Message
of Encouragement

The subject of this chapter represents one of the most strategic
moments in the history of the church. The Holy Spirit emphasized
the importance of this event when He inspired Luke to outline the
circumstances in detail. In Acts 15, we discover a problem, what
caused the problem, how it was solved, and what happened as a
result. In actuality, the solution affected the future history of the
Christian church. Because it was rightly resolved, Christians to this
day who really know the truth have been greatly encouraged—and
can *encourage one another.*

When Paul and Barnabas entered the synagogue in Pisidian
Antioch on their *first* missionary journey, they were asked to share
a "message of encouragement" (Acts 13:15). Paul responded and
delivered a special message which focused on the resurrection of
Jesus Christ (vv. 16-39; see also chap. 7 in this book).

Sometime later, back in Antioch of Syria where their first
missionary tour began and ended, Paul and Barnabas delivered a
second "message of encouragement." This time the focus was on
how a person is saved from sin.

The Problem in Antioch (Acts. 15:1-3)
When Paul and Barnabas returned to Antioch in Syria from their
first church-planting tour, they stayed and ministered. While
there, Luke reports that "Some men came down from Judea to
Antioch and were teaching the brothers: 'Unless you are circum-
cised according to the custom taught by Moses, you cannot be
saved'" (v. 1). Later in the text, we discover that some "Jewish

Christians" were also teaching that a "non-Jewish Christian" must keep the Mosaic law in its entirety in order to have eternal life (v. 5).

The result was disruptive and divisive. Paul and Barnabas, fresh from their missionary journey where numbers of Gentiles had trusted Christ for salvation, did not fade into the woodwork when they observed what was happening. They challenged those men publicly.

The problem, however, was not one they could handle alone. This called for a solution at both "deeper" and "higher" levels. At a deeper level, it demanded a broader theological perspective as to how a person is saved from his sin. At a higher level, the decision had to come from an ecclesiastical body that carried more authority and clout than Paul and Barnabas could muster. Consequently, they and several other key Christians were appointed by the church in Antioch to travel to Jerusalem for advice and counsel.

The Solution in Jerusalem (Acts 15:4-35)

The Report (v. 4). When the delegation from Antioch arrived in Jerusalem they were warmly welcomed by the church and were given opportunity to report what was happening in the Gentile world. This included not only the theological problems in Antioch, but the great response of many Gentiles to the Gospel.

The Pharisees' Response (v. 5). Unfortunately, not everyone agreed with this report—at least in terms of what was actually involved in the Gentiles' conversion experience. In Jerusalem, a number of Pharisees had become believers. However, unlike Paul—who was also a Pharisee—they did not understand God's grace in Christ in relationship to the Law of Moses. They simply added faith in Christ to the tedious system of works they had developed for inheriting eternal life. So they were most concerned that the Gentiles who had responded to the Gospel be required to keep the Mosaic Law, which included circumcision.

Peter's Review (vv. 6-12). Realizing they had a problem that called for careful discussion and deliberation, the "apostles and elders met to consider" these things in a closed session (v. 6). How long this meeting—or these meetings—lasted, we don't know.

Luke simply reports that "after *much discussion,* Peter got up and addressed them" (v. 7).

Peter explained what had happened to him on the rooftop in Joppa and what happened later to Cornelius and his household in Caesarea. Peter's observation was concise: God justified the Gentiles by faith, not by works (v. 9). And his conclusions were twofold:

1. Let's not put a yoke on these Gentile Christians that we Jews cannot even bear. In other words, Peter told the Jewish believers that we should not "try to test God by putting on the necks of the disciples a yoke that neither we nor our fathers have been able to bear" (v. 10).

2. No one, including the Jews, is saved by keeping the law, but by faith. In other words, that's now *we* were saved (v. 11).

It appears that Paul and Barnabas affirmed Peter's report by sharing what they had experienced on their first missionary journey. Everywhere they had seen Cornelius' experience duplicated in the lives of many of the Gentiles. Furthermore, God had indicated His concern for Gentile conversion by working numerous supernatural signs and wonders through these men to confirm the message they were preaching.

James' Reflections (vv. 12-21). James, a top leader in the Jerusalem church, was next to speak. He built his observations and conclusions on both Peter's review and the report shared by Paul and Barnabas. Then he proceeded to point out that what was happening was in harmony with what had been predicted by Old Testament prophets. As an example he cited several statements made by Amos who clearly predicted that Gentiles would be partakers of God's grace (vv. 16-18).

James' conclusion was practical. "We should not make it difficult for the Gentiles who are turning to God," he stated. But because of the numerous Jews living in these large Gentile centers—Jews who had been indoctrinated with the idea that keeping the Law was necessary for salvation—he suggested they write to these Gentile converts and tell them "to abstain from food polluted by idols, from sexual immorality, from the meat of strangled animals, and from blood" (v. 50). These, of course, were not requirements for salvation, but they were to result from their salvation experience.

It is obvious from the rest of the New Testament that some of these requirements were more important and absolute than others—particularly abstaining from sexual immorality. This was never considered an option for a Christian—which became clear in the New Testament literature that later flowed from the pen and lips of men such as Peter, John, Paul, and others.

The Church's Response (vv. 22-29). This rather complex process involved various reports, intense dialogue, some disagreement and prolonged discussion. It eventually resulted in a beautiful unity of thought not only among the apostles and elders in Jerusalem, but also the "whole church" (v. 22). They decided to select two mature and trustworthy men (Judas and Silas) to join Paul and Barnabas in reporting their conclusions to the church in Antioch. In addition, the elders and apostles were told to prepare a letter that could be read, not only to the church in Antioch, but to other Gentile churches who were wrestling with the same issues. With the possible exception of the Epistle to the Galations (which some believe was written by Paul before this Jerusalem letter was penned), this was one of the first letters inspired directly by the Holy Spirit and circulated among the New Testament churches. Luke recorded it in detail. Though short and to the point, it dealt directly with the issues at hand.

> The apostles and elders, your brothers, to the Gentile believers in Antioch, Syria, and Cilicia: Greetings. We have heard that some went out from us without our authorization and disturbed you, troubling your minds by what they said. So we all agreed to choose some men and send them to you with our dear friends Barnabas and Paul—men who have risked their lives for the name of our Lord Jesus Christ. Therefore we are sending Judas and Silas to confirm by word of mouth what we are writing. It seemed good to the Holy Spirit and to us not to burden you with anything beyond the following requirements: You are to abstain from food sacrificed to idols, from blood, from the meat of strangled animals, and from sexual immorality. You will do well to avoid these things (vv. 23-29).

Note that this letter gives no hint that these instructions were required for salvation. Rather, they were exhortations that if practiced, would reflect the Gentile's new life in Christ. The new dietary laws would not cause the Jewish Christians to stumble.

The Results (vv. 30-35). Once this letter was finalized, the four men (Paul, Barnabas, Judas, and Silas) were "sent off" by the Jerusalem church to share it with the Christians in Antioch. "The people read it and *were glad for its encouraging message"* (v. 31).

Why was this letter so encouraging? The answer can be simply stated, first negatively and then positively. Nothing is more *discouraging* than to be involved in a religious system in which you desperately try to do enough to earn your way to heaven, but never know if you measure up to God's standards. Stated positively, these Christians were encouraged because they knew with certainty that their hope rested, not in their ability to keep the Law of Moses, but in their *faith in Jesus Christ.*

In the year 1483, a child was born in Eisleben, Germany who eventually grew up to be a very religious and influential man. In fact, he eventually earned a doctorate of theology degree and for several years lectured at the University of Wittenberg.

During this time, however, this man wrestled with the problem of his own personal sin. He frequently went to confession and faithfully performed the penances. But he never had complete peace regarding his own salvation and relationship to God.

After years of struggling with this issue, he realized through his personal study of Scripture that there was only one answer to his sin problem. He discovered that he could be *justified only by faith* in Christ Jesus, and that no amount of personal good works could ever redeem him. That man was Martin Luther.

The encouragement that came into his soul was like the dawning of a new day. Later he wrote: "It seemed to me as if I had been born again and as if I had entered Paradise through newly opened doors. All at once the Bible began to speak in quite a different way to me. . . . The very phrase 'the righteousness of God,' which I had hated before, was the one that now I loved the best of all." We know, of course, that Luther *was* born again. He had experienced what Jesus had shared with Nicodemus. That new birth resulted from his faith in Christ to be his personal Saviour from sin (John 3:1-21).

As I reflected on Martin Luther's salvation experience, I could not help but think of my own. I remember particularly my early days in high school. I had been reared in a religious group where I was taught that salvation resulted from *both* faith and works. Consequently, when I became a Christian I did all I could to keep the rules of the church, so that I could be approved by God for entrance into heaven. Going to church was really not an encouraging experience for me because I was only reminded of how much more I needed to do to make sure I was eventually saved. Then, one day, I too discovered that my salvation did not depend on my works but on the *finished* work of Jesus Christ. A new sense of joy and encouragement flooded my inner being. I have never been the same since. Though Luther's conversion impacted the world thousands and thousands of times more than mine ever will, we had one thing in common—we were *very encouraged.*

Against this backdrop, and the backdrop of thousands of experiences such as my own, we can understand why the Christians in Antioch felt *so good* about the letter from Jerusalem and why they were encouraged in their hearts. They understood what it meant to be saved by grace through faith.

What About You?

We can learn at least three important lessons from this study. The first we've already stated and illustrated, but let's review it.

1. We are saved by grace through faith, plus nothing (Rom. 4: 1—5:2). This concept is hard for many people to believe. It seems too simple. And yet it is true. Scripture verifies it again and again. In fact, no person has *ever* been saved except in this way, even in Old Testament days.

This is illustrated for us graphically by Paul in his letter to the Roman Christians: "What then shall we say that Abraham, our forefather, discovered in this matter?" asked Paul (4:1). "If, in fact, Abraham was justified by works, he had something to boast about—but not before God" (v. 2).

Paul then asked a second question—"What does the Scripture say?" Again, he answered his own question. "Abraham *believed God,* and it was credited to him as righteousness" (v. 3).

Paul was teaching that Abraham, or any other individual, is saved by faith apart from works. This is clear from his statements to the Romans:

> David says the same thing when he speaks of the blessedness of the man to whom God credits *righteousness apart from works:* "Blessed are they whose transgressions are forgiven, whose sins are covered. Blessed is the man whose sin the Lord will never count against him" (4:6-8).

> He [Abraham] is the father of all *who believe* but have not been circumcised, in order that righteousness might be credited to them. And he is also the father of the circumcised who not only are circumcised but who also walk in the footsteps of *the faith* that our father Abraham had before he was circumcised" (vv. 11-12).

> It was not through law that Abraham and his offspring received the promise that he would be heir of the world, but through the *righteousness that comes by faith*" (v. 13).

> Therefore, since we have been *justified through faith,* we have peace with God through our Lord Jesus Christ, through whom we have gained access *by faith* into this grace in which we now stand. And we rejoice in the hope of the glory of God" (5:1-2).

Philip P. Bliss, a well-known songwriter, understood this truth. He wrote a poem and then set the words to music. And if it had been written early in Christian history, the Christians in Antioch would probably have sung it with gladness when they read the letter from the church in Jerusalem.

> Free from the law—O happy condition!
> Jesus hath bled, and there is remission;
> Cursed by the law and bruised by the fall,
> Grace hath redeemed us once for all.

Now are we free—there's no condemnation!
Jesus provides a perfect salvation;
"Come unto Me—": O hear His sweet call!
Come—and He saves us once for all.

Children of God—O glorious calling!
Surely His grace will keep us from falling;
Passing from death to life at His call,
Blessed salvation—once for all.

Once for all—O sinner, receive it!
Once for all—O brother, believe it!
Cling to the cross, the burden will fall—
Christ has redeemed us once for all!

2. *We are to "work out our salvation" so that Christ's life is reflected in our lives (Eph. 2:8-10; Phil. 2:12-13; Titus 2: 11-12).* Paul dealt with both the first point in this application as well as this second point when he wrote a letter to the Ephesian Christians "For it is by grace you have been saved, *through faith*—and this not from yourselves, it is the gift of God—*not by works,* so that no one can boast" (Eph. 2:8-9).

Paul then speaks to the second point in verse 10, "For we are God's workmanship, *created in Christ Jesus to do good works,* which God prepared in advance for us to do."

To do good works as a Christian, or not to do good works was not the main issue in Antioch. Their main concern was *how* a person is saved. And the answer is that it is by *faith alone.* But in no way are we left with the conclusion that Christians are not to do good works. However, our whole motivation for doing so is different. Again, the Scriptures are clear. Our motivation for obeying God's laws is stated succinctly by Paul in his letter to Titus:

"For the grace of God that brings salvation has appeared to all men. It teaches us to say 'No' to ungodliness and worldly passions, and to live self-controlled, upright, and godly lives in this present age" (Titus 2:11-12).

Shortly after I graduated from Moody Bible Institute in Chicago, I moved to Billings, Montana where I continued my college work and was involved in a Christian radio ministry. I traveled from Chicago to Billings on the Northern Pacific

Railroad, a 24-hour trip. I remember getting on the train in Chicago with a book that someone gave me, entitled *Disciplined by Grace* by J.F. Strombeck (no longer in print but it should be). With plenty of time to read, I completed the book by the time I arrived in Billings. Actually, the book was a careful study of Titus 2:11-12. For a person who had been reared in a legalistic religious system, and "disciplined by rules," the message of that book set me free—not to do what I wanted to do, but to live a holy and righteous life *because* of what God had done for me. It is *because* of His mercy and grace that I presented my body and mind to Christ and determined to conform my life to His and not the world (Rom. 12:1-2). And that has been my goal ever since. Though I have failed God many times, yet He has remained faithful.

It is clear then from Scripture that we are not to "go on sinning so that grace may increase." Rather, under the leadership of the Holy Spirit we are to use our freedom in Christ to live out the "righteous requirements of the law" (8:4). Thus, Paul exhorted the Philippians to "work out your salvation with fear and trembling, for," continued Paul, "it is God who is at work in you, both to will and to work for His good pleasure" (Phil. 2:12-13, NASB).

3. We are never to use our freedom in Christ in such a way that it might cause a weaker Christian to stumble (1 Cor. 8:4-14; Rom. 14:1-23). The Bible clearly outlines those moral and ethical qualities that should characterize a Christlike Christian. "In Christ" we are "a new creation." Therefore, we should walk in the light and not darkness. We should "walk in the light as He [God] is in the light" (1 John 1:7). In his Ephesian letter, Paul is specific. A Christian is to:

- Be truthful (4:25).
- Control anger (v. 26).
- Not steal (v. 28).
- Avoid all sexual immorality (5:3).

The Apostle Paul put it all together when he exhorted Christians to "live a life of love, just as Christ loved us" (5:2). When we do, we are fulfilling the law's requirements (Rom. 13:8-10).

Beyond the specific sins Christians are to avoid, however, there are things in every culture and in every historical situation that are borderline activities. They are not forbidden specifically in Scripture. How can a Christian discern what is appropriate in these circumstances?

This point is illustrated in the letter written to the Christians in Antioch. Eating meat offered to idols was not a sin, nor was partaking of various foods. Paul made this clear in later passages of Scripture. No food is forbidden by God. "Everything God created is good," wrote Paul. "And nothing is to be rejected if it is received with thanksgiving, because it is consecrated by the Word of God and prayer" (1 Tim. 4:4).

On the other hand, Paul recognized a problem with eating "everything" set before a New Testament Christian. A common problem in that day was what to do about food that was first offered to an idol. First of all, Paul stated, "We know that an idol is nothing. . . . But not everyone knows this. Some people are still so accustomed to idols that when they eat such food, they think of it as having been sacrificed to an idol, and since their conscience is weak, it is defiled" (1 Cor. 8:4, 7).

Paul's conclusion then was that our freedom in Christ must "not become a stumbling block to the weak" (v. 9). He spoke to this issue also in Romans 14. Here he instructs both the strong *and* the weak. Christians with strong consciences are to be careful not to hurt Christians with weak consciences. And Christians with weak consciences are not to judge those who may be stronger than they are.

But the fact remains that the primary burden lays on the stronger, more mature Christian. The principle of love should guide and direct our freedom in Christ in areas that are questionable.

Let's take an example. Scripture does not forbid drinking wine. Partaking of this beverage was as culturally acceptable in the New Testament world as coffee is in the 20th-century culture. However, the availability of alcoholic beverages in our culture has created a serious social problem, leading to overindulgence, addiction, and drunkenness.

Does this fact make it wrong to drink a glass of wine? On the basis of Scripture we would have to answer in the negative. However, from Scripture we also have a principle to guide us, for in some situations this may be a serious problem.

Let me illustrate. I received a call one day from a woman who shared a rather shocking story. She had been reading my book,

The Measure of a Woman, (Regal), and had been quite impressed with the chapter where I dealt with the quality of life of "being temperate." Hesitantly, she began to share a pathetic story. Her husband was converted to Christ as an adult out of a life of alcoholism. The Lord miraculously helped him overcome this problem and he eventually became a Christian evangelist.

One day, after several years in the ministry, he was invited to have dinner in the home of a Christian couple. Without any reservation, they served wine at the meal. They, of course, knew nothing of this man's weakness.

Unfortunately, that one exposure was all it took. Two factors were at work. First, as a man who had once been addicted to alcohol, an old pattern was again set in motion. Second, since these Christians were committed to Christ, this man began to rationalize his own behavior. With a broken voice and tears, the woman on the other end of the line told me how her husband once again began drinking. In fact, he often spent the week in a drunken state, sobering up for the weekend so he could participate in various evangelistic ministries in other parts of the country. The process of rationalization had led him into total inconsistency and serious sin.

This story had a strong effect on my own life. Here was a Christian with a weakness who stumbled because of the freedom other Christians took in his presence. I was reminded that there are certain things that may be legitimate in themselves for me to do, but may hurt a weaker Christian. Furthermore, the more responsibility and visibility I have as a Christian leader, the more I must be careful of my Christian example. This is why Paul said, "If what I eat causes my brother to fall into sin, I will never eat meat again, so that I will not cause him to fall" (1 Cor. 8:13).

I have a close friend who attends a Nazarene church in California. The pastor's son is one of the unfortunate people who was held hostage during the Iranian crisis. But from another perspective, this unfortunate situation had a very bright side for this young man. While held in foreign bondage, he became a Christian. Shortly after his son's conversion to Christ, this pastor preached a sermon to his congregation on Jesus' statement in John's Gospel: "If the Son sets you free, you will be free indeed" (John 8:36). He concluded the message with this very moving statement: "Though my son is still a hostage in Iran, since he became a Christian he is more free today than he has ever been before." And this too is the message of Acts 15.

10

Paul's Encouragement Model

When studying the concept of encouragement chronologically in the Book of Acts, the initial focus is clearly on Barnabas. Then Paul enters the scene and joins Barnabas in exemplifying a ministry of encouragement, first in Antioch, and then on the first missionary journey. Even to the casual reader, Barnabas' impact on Paul's life in this area is obvious.

But then something happened. Paul and Barnabas went their separate ways. Ironically, it happened because of a disagreement between these two strong and dynamic men. Paul suggested to Barnabas that they retrace their steps and "visit the brothers in all the towns were we preached the word of the Lord" in order to see how they were progressing in their Christian lives (Acts 15:36). Barnabas agreed, but wanted to take John Mark with them. Paul's response was negative. He had lost confidence in John Mark because he had "deserted them" on their first journey (v. 38). The disagreement was so sharp that they "parted company." Barnabas and John Mark headed for Cyprus, and Paul "chose Silas" and traveled through Syria and Cilicia (vv. 39-40).

From this point in Luke's historical account, the focus shifts primarily to Paul. From a human point of view this is logical for it is clear that for a time Luke also traveled with Paul in a church-planting ministry.

Though these men separated, it is my opinion that Barnabas left a distinct imprint on Paul's life. The once harsh, insensitive and impatient man who had killed Christians because of their faith became a compassionate and sensitive Christian who was willing to lay down his own life for others. Though when compared with Barnabas, who had a distinct "people-orientation," Paul seemed more oriented toward doctrine. Paul *developed* a unique ability to encourage individuals.

Perhaps he reverted more to his old ways of doing things when he rejected John Mark as a traveling companion. If so, he soon regained his focus, which may be reflected when he chose young Timothy to replace Mark (16:1-5). What we know of Paul after this one incident certainly is more reflective of Barnabas' qualities than what Paul himself once was. It was never more obvious than in his ministry in Thessalonica. The most encouraging lesson we see as we study this great apostle's life is that he, like all of us, was in the process of "becoming"—of learning more and more to reflect Jesus Christ in his total lifestyle.

The Founding of the Thessalonican Church
Once Paul and his traveling companions revisited Derbe and then Lystra—where Timothy was invited to join them—they headed further east, eventually arriving in Troas (see map). There Paul had a vision of a man in Macedonia, who was pleading that they come to Europe. Knowing this was from God, they crossed the Aegean Sea. Their first stop was Philippi, where they founded a dynamic church (vv. 11-40). They went on to Thessalonica, and in the midst of persecution founded another church (17:1-9). But the opposition was so keen that they eventually had to leave Thessalonica at night.

However, Paul did not forget these new believers. And as he did so frequently, he followed up his ministry with a letter. It is in this letter we see Paul's continuing ministry of encouragement, both in what he wrote and in his historical reflections.

The Building of the Church
Luke records little in the Book of Acts regarding Paul's specific ministry of encouragement to the believers in Thessalonica. But Paul himself does. The profile he gives us in his first letter to the Thessalonican Christians provides a dynamic model for all believers who want to be encouragers. Let's look at that model.

Gentleness (1 Thes. 2:7). Paul began his reflection on his ministry in Thessalonica in chapter 2. In verse 7 he stated a specific

quality that characterized his life. "As apostles of Christ, we could have been a burden to you," but, said Paul, that was not true. Rather, "we were *gentle* among you, like a mother caring for her little children" (v. 7).

What a contrast! Can this be the same man who several years earlier was "breathing out murderous threats against the Lord's disciples" (Acts 9:1), and *now* used a nursing mother to illustrate his style of ministry? What an example of God's grace! Paul was a changed man—a man of sensitivity and compassion.

It intrigues me that a man so tough, so rigid and unbending reflected this kind of gentleness. No relationship better personifies gentleness than a mother who is nursing a baby. Yet Paul was not ashamed to identify with this analogy. This confirms the depth of change that had taken place in him.

This does not mean that Paul was unwilling to be frank, straightforward, and uncompromising. He never hesitated to confront wrongdoers—especially those whose motives were totally selfish (for example, see Titus 1:10-16). But Paul resorted to this methodology when he saw no hope, or when he saw Christians being deliberately led astray by false teachers. He believed that his initial approach should be a *gentle* one. This is illustrated in his second letter to Timothy: "And the Lord's servant must not quarrel; instead, he must be *kind* to everyone, able to teach, not resentful. Those who oppose him he must *gently instruct,* in the hope that God will grant them repentance leading them to a knowledge of the truth" (2 Tim. 2:24-25).

By the time Paul arrived in Thessalonica, he had learned a great deal about gentleness. And this Timothy observed in Paul's own ministry. With gentleness and tenderness he encouraged these Christians in their new life in Christ.

Self-giving love (1 Thes. 2:8). That Paul became a "people person" is beautifully illustrated in verses 8 and 9. Though he was totally committed to communicating the *message* of Christianity, he knew that message could only be communicated effectively in a context of concern. Thus he wrote, "We loved you so much that we were delighted to share with you not only the Gospel of God [the message] but our *own lives as well,* because you *had become so dear to us"* (v. 8).

Again we see a dramatic contrast! Here's the man who consented to Stephen's martyrdom, now willing to lay down his own life for his fellow Christians. Here is the man who took such a hard line against John Mark now revealing a spirit of concern that truly reflects the very life of Christ Himself.

Pure motives (1 Thes. 2:9). Paul was also an encourager because he was concerned about his motives. He wanted to be trusted. To demonstrate this quality he often gave up his own rights in situations where he felt he could be misinterpreted as being manipulative or on an ego trip or after personal gain. This is why he initially "worked night and day" in Thessalonica. Many false teachers throughout the first-century world were taking financial advantage of their followers. Consequently, Paul would not accept gifts from people till they understood his motives. He did not want to be classified as this kind of man. Consequently, he "never used flattery," nor did he "put on a mask to cover up greed" (v. 5).

Consistency (1 Thes. 2:10). Paul tried hard to practice what he preached. He hesitated to ask people to do something he was not willing to do himself. In fact, he often did things he did not insist that others do, simply because of his prominent position as a

Christian leader. Consequently, he could write to these believers, "You are witnesses, and so is God, of how *holy, righteous* and *blameless* we were among you who believed" (v. 10). No one could accuse Paul of inconsistent Christian behavior.

Personalization (1 Thes. 2:11-12). Why was Paul so successful in his ministry? The final verses in this paragraph make it even more clear. He did not teach people as "groups" but as individuals. And his final point rounds out the family illustration begun in verse 7. Not only was he serving as a "nursing mother" to these people, but as a "father," who dealt with *each one* personally— *"encouraging, comforting,* and *urging"* them "to live lives worthy of God" (v. 12). Paul's gentleness, self-giving love, pure motives, and consistent Christian example were positive, at a personal level—like a father with his children.

The importance of this example for today's fathers was captured in a letter written to Ann Landers. The headline read: "Dad, Name of Game is 'Gentleness.'"

Dear Ann Landers: This letter has been written in my head a hundred times. Now it goes on paper and into the mailbox. It is called: "Games Fathers Play."

Pinning: This is a game where the father wants to hold his son down. Son tires after a few minutes, but father persists. After a few more minutes, son screams to be freed, or cries or begs, but father just smiles and berates the boy for being a sissy.

Score: Daddy 10, Son 0.

Boxing: This is a game of self-defense. A few punches, a push, a shove, a loud command to fight back "like a man." Son whimpers—feels inadequate, knows the odds are against him. So he cries. Father teases him for being a sissy.

Score: Daddy 10, Son 0.

Football: This is a game of skill and kill. Son must have killer instinct at 6 years of age. He must outshine all others and give 110 percent. Daddy gets very angry if son doesn't make the team or turn out to be a star.

Score: Daddy 10, Son 0.

Now, Daddy, after all your guidance and nurturing, son grows to manhood. He is the image of *you*—his instructor and role model. He is critical, abusive, and insecure. The score is Daddy 0, Son 0.

This is the story of my son and his father. I say to you dads everywhere that one of the most precious games you can play with your son is "Gentleness," but in a manly way. A kiss, a hug, an approving glance and some kind words. He is sure to become a man among men if you play this game.
    Score: Daddy 10, Son 10.
Sign me.

—The Scorekeeper

Dear Scorekeeper: I agree with your observations completely. Thank you for mailing the letter. It packed a real wallop. And now, Dad, if your wife hands you this column, don't get mad. Get smart (*Ann Landers, Field Newspaper Syndicate, The Kansas City Star,* June 15, 1980, p. 2C).

Imitating Paul Today

Paul deeply desired to be a worthy model. Though he acknowledged his weaknesses and his limitations, he could write to the Corinthians without apology and encourage them by saying, "Follow my example, as I follow the example of Christ" (See 1 Cor. 4:16). We too can be encouragers—just like Paul. His style of ministry illustrates how.

1. We must be gentle. The quality of gentleness is powerful in dealing with people of all ages. It can soften the heart of a child as well as an adult. It can create beautiful memories and it can dissipate anger. That is why the proverb states: "A gentle answer turns away wrath" (Prov. 15:1).

Some of my most vivid memories, even as a child, relate to how people dealt with my weaknesses. I remember a specific incident that happened when I was in first grade. The teacher, Olive Owens, had outlined the word *me* in a beautiful cursive style on the chalkboard. She then told us to copy the word on our papers.

I had never written a word in my life. Those were pre-

Sesame Street days! Try as I might, I couldn't get my pencil to cooperate.

To my dismay, Miss Owens began to look at each student's work—one by one. I was in the third row of seats. She completed row one, came up row two, and then started down row three. My heart was pounding. What would she think of my inability? What would she do? These were pressing questions in my six-year-old heart.

And then there she was, looking straight down at my paper and a few marks that resembled more the work of a runaway seismograph than the efforts of a six-year-old boy. My heart was pounding even more and I was so overwhelmed with fear that I broke into tears.

At that moment, Miss Owens did something that I'll never forget. She leaned over, and with a compassionate voice said, "That's alright, Gene." Then she sealed her words with a kiss on my cheek.

To this day I remember that gentle moment. It dispelled my fears and gave me courage to try again. I'm convinced that my teacher's gentleness helped me to take a giant step in the direction of liking school, rather than hating it.

There are other moments I remember too—some not so pleasant. One is very distinct. I must have been about eight years old. I was at church, and the main service had just begun. There's no question but that I was engaging in behavior that was inappropriate. I was involved in a footrace with another boy—up and down the stairway in the main lobby.

There was a man in the church who took it upon himself to correct me. In the midst of my footrace, this large hand reached out and grabbed me by the hair. (For those of you who have seen me, this incident may explain some things). I suddenly screeched to a halt—but under some very uncomfortable conditions.

Today I still remember the angry look on the man's face, and the disgust that controlled his countenance. I still remember the feelings of fear that came over me. Throughout my years of growing up in that community, those feelings and memories lingered.

It is true that I needed discipline. My parents were also probably at fault in allowing me too much freedom. But it is also true that the punishment did not match the crime, and I knew it even as a child. I sensed I was a victim of a very angry man. There was no gentleness, only hardness and insensitivity. As I grew up I began to realize that hardness and insensitivity might have been all he knew.

A gentle spirit *is* powerful. Even as adults we respond accordingly. In that sense we never grow away from responding positively to gentleness and negatively to harshness and insensitivity. The facts are that we can encourage or discourage people with our tone of voice. I confess this is something I must work at consistently.

2. We must be self-giving. We are living in a self-centered society. Paul was willing to give his life so that others might find Christ. Today many people are not willing to walk across the street to help someone else, let alone die for them.

Unfortunately, this mentality can creep into the Christian community. We can be selfish and egocentric too. In fact, some non-Christians are seemingly more interested in other people than some Christians are. That of course is a tragedy.

But let's be positive. There are many Christians who *are* self-giving. Many of them have crossed my own path. In my life they have become the most encouraging people I know. I want to be with them and I want to be like them. They make me feel good all over.

I think of one couple in my own church. There's no question that they are self-giving people. I see it in their husband/wife relationship. I sense it in their relationship with their children. It is obvious in their hospitality. I see it in their concern for others in the church. I sense it in their use of time. I see it in their use of money. If I ever had a serious problem that I could share with no one else, I feel I could share it with them. The most encouraging thing is, I know others like them. They're Christians, and they're my friends. That is indeed encouraging!

3. We must keep our motives pure. This is a difficult challenge. For one thing, it is tough to have totally pure motives. Sometimes it is hard to tell what our motives really are. But there are ways to work in the direction of pure motives. Consider these questions:

- *Do I love others unconditionally?* If we find ourselves primarily "giving" to "get," we'll get angry when others do not respond to what we are doing for them. That's a sure clue something's wrong in our innermost being. I've sensed that reaction in my own life, and it has brought me up short— made me question my motives. And sure enough, my motives were more selfish than unselfish.

On the other hand this does not mean that we should be doormats, letting others walk all over us. But it *does* mean we should attempt to understand people who take advantage of us—or others—and look on them with compassion rather than intense dislike.

• *Do I reach out to others to help them?* If our motives are pure, we will not be terribly hurt and feel rejected if people do not reciprocate.

• *What am I willing to sacrifice to help others succeed?* The degree to which we are willing to do so is a clue to understanding *why* we do what we do.

4. We must strive to be consistent. The direct meaning of Paul's statement in 1 Thessalonians 2:10 relates to consistent Christian living; that is, living up to what we profess.

I was listening one day to an interview on a Christian radio station with a non-Christian college student. The interviewer asked a young woman what she thought of her fellow students who claimed to be Christians. Her immediate response was that she felt they did not live up to their profession of faith. For example, she said, "Some of them have bumper stickers on their cars that say 'Honk, if you love Jesus.' And they cut you off on the expressway just like everyone else." (If you knew anything about my driving habits, you'd know why I felt guilty after hearing her straightforward indictment!) Her concluding remark was she wanted to *see* Christianity—not just *hear* about it.

Granted, some non-Christians are overly critical. They need to read the bumper sticker that says, "Christians are not perfect; just forgiven." But on the other hand, many of us *are* inconsistent in areas we ought not to be.

The inconsistency principle also applies to our moods and our dispositions. Most of us experience anxiety when we are with people who are kind one day and harsh the next; unselfish one day and selfish the next; people who are emotionally up one day and down the next. Often their expressions of love reflect either feast or famine. They either lavish it on you or give you nothing.

Of course, we all have our moody moments. I am sure I often create anxiety in others because of my own inconsistency. We can't be totally consistent. Even Jesus' moods fluctuated. But He was characterized by an overall consistency. His fluctuating emotions were related to legitimate concerns and causes. If we want to be encouragers, we must follow His example.

5. *We must be person-oriented.* Obviously it is impossible to relate on an intimate personal level with everyone we know. But we should not be aloof and removed either. To achieve this goal we must stop thinking of "groups" and think of "individuals" in those groups. We must stop thinking about "crowds" and think about individual people in those crowds. We must stop thinking of "classes" and "congregations" and think of people with needs, people who are different and unique in their own right. We must stop thinking so much about ourselves and think more of others.

I have a friend who was an extremely busy person during the prime of his life. Everyone wanted his attention. Because people felt he cared, he was inundated with requests for help and counsel. People just wanted to talk to him, to be with him. But in all of his busyness, he seldom let you feel that he was too busy for you—even if he couldn't stop and talk or spend time with you.

That's an art! I wish I had it. But we can all try. We can be person-oriented, particularly in the sphere of people who work with us. We can practice it in our families and in our small groups—but particularly in our families. We can develop an attitude that *conveys* concern even when we can't personally *do* something about *everyone's* needs.

Life Response

Every Christian is to be an encourager. And this is an ongoing experience. It is not achieved overnight nor is it achieved once for all! Where are you in the process?

On a scale of 1 to 10, how would you rate yourself? As you do, try to think through all of your human relationships—with your mate, your children, your friends, your fellow employees, etc.

Never   *Always*
1 2 3 4 5 6 7 8 9 10   1. I am a gentle person.
1 2 3 4 5 6 7 8 9 10   2. I am self-giving.
1 2 3 4 5 6 7 8 9 10   3. I have proper motives.
1 2 3 4 5 6 7 8 9 10   4. I am a consistent Christian.
1 2 3 4 5 6 7 8 9 10   5. I am person-oriented.
NOTE: If you are married, ask your spouse to rate you.

Select the quality you are strongest in and thank God for that quality. Then select the quality where you need the most improvement. Think of one way you can practice that quality. Then ask God to help you carry out your goal.

This week and with God's help I will:

_____

_____

_____

11

Encouraging One Another with Words

During the limited time Paul ministered in Thessalonica, he and his co-workers had given these new Christians an intensive course in Christian doctrine, with an emphasis on the second coming of Jesus Christ (2 Thes. 2:5). But once they left the church, because of persecution, Paul's concern for their spiritual welfare prompted him to send Timothy back to visit them in order to "strengthen and encourage" them in their faith (1 Thes. 3:1-2).

Timothy's report to Paul was positive and encouraging. These new believers *were* "standing firm in the Lord" (v. 8). However, there were two important aspects of the second coming of Jesus Christ they did not yet fully understand.

Hope for Those Who Have Died
Though the Thessalonican Christians understood that Jesus Christ was going to return to take them to heaven, they did not really know what would happen to Christians who died *before* Christ's return. Evidently some of their Christian friends and loved ones had already passed away since Paul's initial ministry in Thessalonica and they were very concerned about their eternal destiny.

Paul dealt with this question in his first letter. "We do not want you to be ignorant about those who sleep [that is those who have died]," Paul wrote, "or to grieve like the rest of men, who have no hope" (1 Thes. 4:13). Then Paul gave the reason they should not grieve in this way: "We believe that Jesus died and rose again and so we believe that God will bring with Jesus those who have fallen asleep in Him" (v. 14).

There was no question that the Thessalonican Christians believed that Jesus Christ was going to return from heaven to take them to be with Him (1:10). In fact, they were eagerly looking for Him to return in their lifetime. Unlike most Christians today, they did not anticipate dying before the event transpired.

Dealing with their fears, Paul made it clear that *all* believers—dead or alive—would be part of the rapture. "The dead in Christ will rise first," he reassured them, and then "after that, we who are still alive and are left will be caught up with them in the clouds to meet the Lord in the air" (4:17). To make sure they understood this matter clearly, he stated: "And so we will be with the Lord *forever*" (v. 17).

You can imagine the encouragement these words brought to those New Testament Christians and the emotional excitement that flooded their hearts when they heard this. Some were no doubt grieving deeply over the loss of their loved ones—a loss that itself is difficult to face. But to face this loss not knowing for sure what would happen to their loved ones certainly intensified their grief. In many respects, without proper theological knowledge they had no more hope than their pagan counterparts. This was why Paul told them they need not "grieve like *the rest of men* who have no hope" (v. 13b). They were different! Grief, yes! That's natural. But not like those who are not Christians.

When a Christian Dies

I had the great privilege of preaching my dad's funeral. I had not seen him for several months when we received word of his death. He died at age 78, doing what he loved—driving the tractor on the family farm in Indiana. He suffered a heart attack and the tractor swerved off into some pine trees. The engine died and my mother found him still sitting on the tractor seat with his hands quietly resting on his lap.

When my own family received word of his death, we immediately flew to Indiana for the funeral. I remember walking into the funeral home where his body was available for viewing. When I first saw him, my heart was instantly filled with grief. There lay my father. Tears welled up in my eyes and it was difficult for me to accept the fact that he was no longer alive. At that moment I wished I had been able to have had just one more conversation with him.

But as I passed through those initial minutes of grief, I remembered what we had talked about so often when we were together—the hope we both had in Jesus Christ. He particularly enjoyed talking about the second coming of Christ. My grief began to subside as I realized that my father was not really residing in the body I was viewing. In a sense Christ "had already come" for him. More accurately, of course, he had gone to be with Christ which Paul said, was far better than to remain on earth (Phil. 1:23).

As I reached out to touch him, I knew I was only touching the "home" he had lived in for 78 years. My dad's soul was in heaven with Jesus—and far better off at that moment than I was. In the midst of my own tears I was sure he was in that place where there were no tears—only eternal joy and happiness. Some day God would bring him "with Jesus" to take all those who are yet alive to be with the Lord forever. Together the "dead in Christ" and "those who are still alive" would be "caught up . . . in the clouds to meet the Lord in the air" (1 Thes. 4:16-17). My dad's soul would be reunited with his body—a new body. Once again we would be able to converse together, but this time in the presence of the Lord.

Did that truth make any difference at that moment in my life? All the difference in the world—for me and my whole family! That knowledge and understanding enabled me to calmly stand before a large audience of people the next day and preach his funeral message. There I announced with all certainty that my dad had gone home to be with the Lord Jesus Christ. I was not grieving like those who had no hope! Nor was my family.

Paul told the Thessalonican Christians to "encourage each other with these words" (v. 18). That's what I was doing that day for the Christians I knew in my own hometown. Paul was not denying there would be sorrow over the death of loved ones. Rather, he was telling them their grief was different. Their separation was only temporary. They would be united again when Jesus Christ comes to take *all* His children home to heaven—those who have died and those who are still alive.

When a Non-Christian Dies

I have conducted funerals for people who were not ready to face eternity; those who died not knowing Jesus Christ as personal

Saviour and Lord. And none of those—family or friends—who were left behind knew Jesus Christ as Saviour.

What a contrast! There is really very little to say by way of encouragement. I have only been able to be there and try to comfort those who mourn. Though I have shared Scripture—such as Psalm 23—I have known in my heart that it is really not applicable to their situation. When there is no eternal hope, there is grief beyond compare!

One day I was flying to Denver and seated beside me was a young woman. Something seemed to be bothering her and she was often on the verge of tears. As we talked together, I soon discovered that her mother had died from cancer. The event was still fresh in her mind and she was grieving deeply.

I also discovered she was Jewish. This made it relatively easy to share with her at a spiritual level. We talked a great deal about the intricate relationships between Judaism and Christianity. I think she was rather surprised at my love for the Old Testament.

Toward the end of our conversation I shared with her that I felt that her own heart seemed to be very open to learning more about Jesus Christ, who I believe is the true Messiah. Tears welled up in her eyes. Then she asked me two difficult questions. "What happens when we die? Can we really know for sure what happens?"

What a privilege it was to share with her that we *can* know what happens if we know Jesus Christ as the true Messiah. Though she did not respond in faith at that time, she promised she would study more about this matter.

Here was a girl without hope. She had stared death in the face. Since her mother was very close to her, she was grieving deeply because she could not answer those hard questions. But for the Christian, there *is* hope. We can know what happens when we die.

By way of contrast, let me share another illustration. I met a pastor and his wife several years ago while speaking at a special conference in Wisconsin. One afternoon they took me waterskiing. At that time they had a young son named Mikey who had a congenital heart disease. He was with us that afternoon in the boat and was a great little fellow. Though he had to remain quite inactive, it was obvious that he was very special.

Several months later, I received a letter from this couple. What they wrote moved me deeply.

. . . As you might recall Mikey had heart surgery in September of '78. Although he had a few bright spots since then, generally it was downhill. We lost him last October 30th. . . . He died on the operating table, *before* they could begin the surgery. The doctor said, "I've never seen anything quite like it. Your son looked around the room, sighed, closed his eyes and his heart stopped. We couldn't make it start up again."

We weren't surprised. Mikey's death, like his life was a miracle to be a part of. The morning before he died, he asked, "Daddy, if I don't live after my surgery and I get to go to be with Jesus, how will I get there? Will He give me wings? Will I be able to talk to Noah? How long will I have to wait until you come to be with me?"

We walked Mikey down the hall to the elevator leading up to the operating room and he turned to Ruth and said, "Mommie, it's going to seem like a long wait for you, but for me it will be easy. I'm just going to go in there and go to sleep." And that's exactly what he did. . . . We miss him greatly, but God has given us peace and comfort.

Mikey had hope! And every person who knows Jesus Christ as Saviour has hope beyond the grave. This is what Paul meant when he said, "Encourage each other with these words" (1 Thes. 4:18).

Hope for Those Who Live

Paul also encouraged the Thessalonians by answering a second question: What happens to those Christians who are alive when God's judgment comes upon the earth—a period of time which is identified in the Bible as "the Day of the Lord"? It will come, Paul wrote "like a thief in the night" (1 Thes. 5:2). In fact, people will be saying that everything is great and then it will happen. "Destruction will come on them suddenly . . . and they will not escape" (v. 3).

Paul explained again what he had taught them. That "day" should not surprise them for they would be delivered from that great period of judgment on the earth. "We do not belong to the night or to the darkness," Paul wrote (vv. 4-5), "we belong to the day" and we have "the *hope* of salvation" (v. 8). To make sure they understood clearly, Paul made his point once again. "For

God did not appoint us to *suffer wrath* but to receive salvation through our Lord Jesus Christ. He died for us so that, whether we are awake or asleep, we may live together with Him" (vv. 9-10).

Personally, I believe Paul is explaining that as Christians we will not experience that terrible period of Tribulation that is so graphically described in the Book of Revelation. I believe Christians will be caught up to be with Christ before it takes place.

On one occasion I was speaking at a special conference in Alaska. I asked about the various religious groups that existed there. I was informed that some "Christians" there had settled in one of the most unpopulated areas of that state and were carefully preparing for the great tribulation. They were storing up food supplies, building underground shelters, and generally preparing for the Day of the Lord.

I do not believe this kind of behavior reflects the hope Paul was talking about in 1 Thessalonians 5. I do not know of any instructions in Scripture that tell us to prepare for the Day of the Lord in this way. Rather, we are to be spiritually ready while we wait for the "blessed hope" (Titus 2:13). It is with these promises of deliverance from *God's wrath* we are to "encourage one another and build each other up" (1 Thes. 5:11).

Don't misunderstand. I'm not suggesting that as 20th-century Christians living in the United States we will not suffer persecution. The Thessalonicans were already suffering persecution (3:2-4). So have thousands of Christians throughout the history of the church. Many have been put to death for their faith in Christ. In many parts of the world today, Christians *continue* to suffer persecution.

No, Paul is not teaching that Christians will be spared persecution. Rather, he is teaching that we will be delivered from God's judgment on this earth when He pours out His wrath on unbelieving mankind because of their sin and unwillingness to repent. This is the hope we have in Christ. Even if we are alive when Christ comes for the church, we will escape the judgment that follows. "Therefore," Paul wrote, *"encourage one another* and build each other up, just as in fact you are doing" (5:11). In other words, keep on doing what you're doing and do it even more.

Encouraging One Another with Words

The focus of Paul's exhortations to "encourage one another" in the Thessalonian epistle is on words of truth regarding the second coming of Jesus Christ. In addition to correct doctrine, there are many other word messages we can use to encourage one another. When we use them appropriately, they have a profound impact on those who hear them. Let's look at some of the things that happen as stated in the Book of Proverbs.

> **An anxious heart weighs a man down, but a kind word cheers him up (Prov. 12:25).**

At times all of us have experienced the kind of anxiety spoken about in this proverb. It's that heavy feeling that comes over us when we are deeply troubled about something. It may be caused by a family illness or the death of a close friend or loved one. For one of many reasons, we might be disappointed in ourselves. We have inadvertently hurt someone's feelings or let someone down. We may have failed to achieve some goal that was important to us. Or we may be disappointed in someone else who has let us down.

There are many reasons for a heavy heart. I remember one experience when I felt terribly confused. I could literally feel the weight in my chest. Obviously, my internal organs did not increase in size. But my feelings of grief and anxiety were so real that I felt heaviness in my chest.

This is why the "heart" is frequently used by biblical writers as a focal point for emotions—whether they are positive or negative. Penning the Psalms, David wrote, "You have *filled my heart with greater joy* than when their gain and new wine abound" (Ps. 4:7). "My *heart rejoices* in your salvation" (13:5). Because of God's protection in his life, he said, "Therefore *my heart is glad*" (16:9).

On the other hand David reminded us that "the Lord is close to the *brokenhearted* and saves those who are crushed in spirit" (34:18). And on one occasion when he was in deep despair, he wrote—"I am feeble and utterly crushed; I groan in *anguish of heart*" (38:8).

In Proverbs 12:25, Solomon is referring to the effects of a heavy heart. But he also shares with us how that anxiety and heaviness can be dissipated. A *kind word* can cheer us up.

To what extent are you encouraging people with kind words? Don't withhold that which is so powerful, so effective, so biblical.

Every once in awhile I receive a letter from someone who has been especially encouraged by my ministry—either through a particular message or through reading one of my books. It's *always* a thrill—always encouraging. It's especially encouraging if it comes at a time when I'm feeling low or downhearted. Oftentimes it's this kind "word of encouragement" that motivates me to go on and repeat the process in someone else's life. I thank God for those words of encouragement.

One day a close friend of mine came into my office. "Gene," he said, "you've helped me greatly in my own life. And I want you to know that I want to help you anytime I can."

Sensing that my heart was heavy, he said something very perceptive. His concern encouraged me. Our time together was brief, but knowing his concern helped me through that particular day.

As I reflected on that conversation, I came across this verse: "A happy heart makes the face cheerful, but heartache crushes the spirit" (Prov. 15:13). What we are "inside" *does* make a difference on the "outside." His perceptions were accurate, and I'm glad he encouraged me.

To what extent are you healing broken hearts? You can! Just remember: "An anxious heart weighs a man down, but a kind word cheers him up" (12:25).

Pleasant words are a honeycomb, sweet to the soul and healing to the bones (Prov. 16:24).

This second proverb is closely related to the one we just looked at, but it treats another important dimension of encouragement. In this verse Solomon writes about pleasant words and likens them to sweetness of honey.

My sister, as an adult, enjoys the stories of Winnie the Pooh. If you're aware of these cute little stories, you already know that Pooh's favorite pastime is to put his head in the honey jar.

This is a beautiful analogy. Unless we're somewhat abnormal, we all—unfortunately—enjoy sweet things. And, wrote Solomon, pleasant words are sweet things.

But notice their effect. They are "sweet to the *soul* and healing to the *bones.*" Man is basically a two dimensional creature—both soul/spirit and body. To put it another way, we are both psychological beings and physical beings. And, of course, both are interrelated, so much so that we often talk about experiencing "psychosomatic" conditions. The first part of this word, *psycho,* comes from the Greek word *psychē,* meaning soul. The second part of the word, *somatic,* comes from the Greek word *sōma* meaning body. Therefore, *psychosomatic* refers to both the soul and body. Solomon reminds us that pleasant words affect both our psychological and physiological being in a positive way. These kinds of words have good psychosomatic effects on us.

On the other hand, Solomon also reminds us the opposite is true. He also penned this proverb, "A cheerful heart is good medicine, but a crushed spirit dries up the bones" (Prov. 17:22).

I am reminded of several students who decided they were going to test this idea. Together they agreed to give one of their friends negative feedback regarding his mental and physical well being. Soon after this decision, one of the students met the young man in the hallway at the start of the day. "What's wrong, John?" he asked.

"What do you mean?" John replied. "I'm OK. In fact I feel great!"

"Oh, really, John," the student replied. "You don't look very well."

Several minutes later, a second student met John. "Hey," he said, "you don't look well. What's wrong?"

"Well, actually," John replied, "I feel fine . . . I think."

Later a third student met John. "You really don't look well," he said.

"Yeah," said John. "I don't feel good at all. I think I'd better go home and go to bed. I'm really quite sick."

This may be a bit humorous—and rather unkind—but it illustrates Solomon's point well. "Pleasant words are a honeycomb, sweet to the soul and healing to the bones" (Prov. 16:24). But on the other hand, "A cheerful heart is good medicine, but a crushed spirit dries up the bones" (17:22).

To what extent are you healing broken spirits? You can. Or, are you one of those people who enjoys "breaking spirits," and discouraging people? There are people, even Christians, with this philosophy of life. How sad! And what a commentary on their own happiness. Be a "healer," not a "hurter." An important means to that end is very clear—use *pleasant words.*

A word aptly spoken is like apples of gold in settings of silver (Prov. 25:11).

I especially like this proverb. It demonstrates the importance of choosing our words carefully and sharing them at the right times.

One day a friend and I were riding our motorcycles in the mountains. We were following a winding dirt trail, and suddenly we looked out ahead. There rising majestically into the sky was one of the most beautiful Spanish peaks in southern Colorado. We pulled our motorcycles to a stop and drank in the beauty.

Then I noticed what made the mountain so captivating. It was naturally framed by a long hanging branch above us. To our left was a sloping cliff that formed the frame on that side. Rising up from the mountainside were some gorgeous trees on the right. To "top it off" the clouds above the mountain were hovering at just the right angle. Actually, that beautiful Spanish peak looked just like "apples of gold in settings of silver."

Solomon said that words spoken in the right circumstances at the right time are just as captivating and memorable as that mountain. I'll never forget that scene as long as I live. I can remember words that are just as vivid. I'm sure you can too.

Are you using your potential to encourage others? You should. It is a skill that every one of us can develop. In fact, it usually doesn't come naturally. It takes practice.

Understand, of course, that Solomon was not talking about flattery. This kind of communication is used with false motives. But words spoken in proper ways are primarily for the benefit of the hearer—not for the one who has uttered the words.

Life Response

Think about your use of words. *First,* think of someone you can encourage. The following suggestions will help you pinpoint someone in need:

- Think of someone who is spiritually confused.
- Think of someone who is discouraged.
- Think of someone who is suffering from fear.

- Think of someone who is anxious.
- Think of someone who is physically ill.
- Think of someone under great pressure.
- Think of someone who is always "giving out" to others.
- Think of someone who is failing at a task or who has already failed.
- Think of someone who is lonely.

Second, what can you say to encourage this person? Formulate a basic idea:

Third, how will you say it?

By letter.

By phone.

Person to person.

By tape.

Other. _____

12

The God
of All Comfort

This final chapter in our study focuses on who—in the final analysis—is the ultimate Source of *all* encouragement. As we will clearly see from Paul's experience, though God is that ultimate Source, His primary *means* for encouraging us involves other Christians.

In our last two chapters, both Paul's "encouragement model" and his use of *words* to encourage others involved the Thessalonian Christians. Our final look at the theme of encouraging one another follows naturally the geographical and sequential pattern we have looked at all along in the Book of Acts.

When Paul and his fellow missionaries left Thessalonica on the second missionary journey, they went on to Berea (Acts 17:10), then to Athens (v. 15), and eventually to Corinth (18:1). Because of their ministry, the church at Corinth was born (see map, chap. 10).

The Corinthians were in some respects unique people in the New Testament world. They were definitely some of the most morally degenerate. Temple prostitution was rampant, and because Corinth was also a seaport town, moral perversion pervaded the city.

When some of these people came to Christ, it took a while for them to shed their old lifestyle and begin to reflect their new life in Christ. When Paul left the church a year and a half later (18:11), he left behind a group of Christians who were still some of the most immature and carnal believers in the New Testament world (1 Cor. 3:1-4).

With this in mind, we can understand more clearly the nature of the Corinthian letters. They are filled with references to this carnality. Evidently Paul also wrote a third letter that is not included in the Bible (see 1 Cor. 5:9). The third letter was even more direct and exhortatory than the two that are included.

One of the most predominant themes included in this second letter, however, is that of encouragement. In fact, Paul introduces the letter with this idea and in 5 brief verses he uses the Greek word *paraklēsis* 10 times. Most scholars translate this word "comfort." R.V.G. Tasker reminds us that "this word perhaps better than any other conveys the double meaning of 'encouragement' and 'consolation' inherent in the Greek word *Paraklēsis"* (*The Second Epistle of Paul to the Corinthians,* Eerdmans, p. 41). Nevertheless, this is the same basic concept we've encountered all along in the Book of Acts and the epistles that were written to the various churches. Let's look more carefully at how Paul uses the concept of "encouragement" or "comfort" when writing to the Corinthians.

Paul's Troubles

After Paul's initial greeting, he immediately offers thanksgiving and praise to God for His help and encouragement during the periods of discouragement and difficulty. Thus we read, "Praise be to the God and Father of our Lord Jesus Christ, the Father of compassion and the God of all comfort, who comforts us in all our *troubles"* (2 Cor. 1:3-4).

Paul's life and ministry were often characterized by extreme difficulties. Regarding his ministry in Asia, he informed the Corinthians that he and his co-workers "were under great pressure." These pressures, he continued, were "far beyond our ability to endure, so that we despaired even of life. Indeed, in our hearts we felt the sentence of death" (vv. 8-9).

This kind of persecution and suffering was not new in the lives of these New Testament missionaries. Later, in this same letter Paul referred to the fact that they often experienced "troubles, hardships, and distresses; in beatings, imprisonments, and riots; hard work, sleepless nights, and hunger" (6:4-5). He further elaborated on the nature of these problems in chapter 11, particularly as they involved his own life.

> Five times I received from the Jews the 40 lashes minus one. Three times I was beaten with rods, once I was stoned, three times I was shipwrecked, I spent a night and a day in the open sea, I have been constantly on the move. I have been in danger from rivers, and danger from bandits, and danger from my own countrymen, and danger from Gentiles; and danger in the city, and danger in the country, and danger at sea . . . I have labored and toiled and have often gone without sleep; I have known hunger and thirst and have often gone without food; I have been cold and naked (11:24-27).

Following this specific list of experiences that involves intensive physical suffering, Paul referred to his greatest psychological burden: "Besides everything else, I face daily the pressure of *my concern for all the churches*" (v. 28). Founding churches in the midst of persecution and other hardships was only the beginning of Paul's difficulties. His pastoral heart was continually burdened and concerned for the spiritual welfare of the believers who were scattered throughout the New Testament world.

Paul's Comfort

In the midst of "all of our troubles"—both physical and psychological—Paul wrote, "The God of *all comfort . . . comforts us*" (2 Cor. 1:3).

How did this take place? How did God comfort and encourage Paul and his fellow missionaries? It may appear that this was some kind of mystical and mysterious spiritual uplift, involving only God and these spiritual leaders, that cannot be isolated and defined. Not so! Throughout this letter Paul outlines clearly the *means* God used to encourage him and his co-workers. Let's look at these factors, and for the sake of simplicity, let's focus in on the Apostle Paul himself.

1. Paul saw a special purpose in his troubles. The apostle first of all outlines for us that he was encouraged because he knew he could directly identify with the trouble of other Christians and comfort them just as he had been comforted by the Lord (1:4). This in itself was a significant source of encouragement. "For just as the sufferings of Christ flow over into our lives, so also through Christ our *comfort* overflows. If we are distressed, it is for your *comfort* and salvation; if we are *comforted,* it is for your *comfort,* which produces in you patient endurance of the same sufferings we suffer" (vv. 5-6).

Paul gained physical, psychological, and spiritual strength just knowing his own suffering and God's help in the midst of that suffering would enable him to help others. He saw purpose and meaning in his difficulties. He credited God for being the Source of his ability to see that kind of purpose in his own time of stress.

2. *Paul was encouraged by the prayers of fellow Christians.* As we have already seen, Paul was often in situations that endangered his life. Again and again he was delivered through placing his total confidence in God and on the prayers of his Christian friends. "On Him we have set our hope," he wrote, "that He will continue to deliver us, *as you help us by your prayers.* Then," Paul continued, "many will give thanks on our behalf for the gracious favor granted us *in answer to the* prayers of many" (1:10-11).

Paul relied heavily on prayer support from those who knew him and loved him, not only for protection from his enemies, but that he might be effective in his ministry. Writing to the Ephesians, he said, "Pray also for me . . . that I will fearlessly make known the mystery of the Gospel, for which I am an ambassador in chains. *Pray* that I may declare it fearlessly as I should" (Eph. 6:19-20).

Writing from his Roman prison cell, Paul voiced his confidence to the Philippians. "Yes, and I will continue to *rejoice,* for I know that through your *prayers* and the help given by the Spirit of Jesus Christ, what has happened to me will turn out for my deliverance" (Phil. 1:18-19).

There was no question that prayer was an important reason why Paul experienced God's encouragement and comfort. Again and again he was protected, not from suffering itself, but from physical death. This involved God's direct intervention in his life.

3. *Paul was encouraged by his eternal perspective.* God's special comfort and encouragement in Paul's life was related to what He had provided for Paul (and all Christians) in the future. No matter what happened to him physically, this man knew he had an

eternal home. "Therefore," he said, "we do not lose heart." His eternal perspective is what kept Paul from giving up. "Though *outwardly* we are wasting away," he wrote, "yet *inwardly* we are being renewed day by day. For our light and *momentary troubles* are achieving for us an eternal glory that far outweighs them all" (2 Cor. 4:16-17).

Even if God chose to allow Paul to lose his life, he took great comfort in knowing he would be with Jesus Christ. In fact, when he wrote to the Philippians, he knew his chances of being executed were great. That is why he said "for to me, to live is Christ and to die is gain" (Phil. 1:21). As we have seen from an earlier quotation, he was rejoicing in his situation no matter what, for he was convinced that he would be *delivered* (v. 19).

It is important at this point to understand what Paul meant by "deliverance." It had a twofold meaning for him. Either he would be "delivered" from prison to spend more time with the Philippian Christians, or he would be "delivered" from faltering in his Christian testimony as he faced the threat of death at the hands of the emperor. In actuality, there was a third alternative, for if his life were taken, then he would be "delivered" from his earthly "home" to spend eternity with Christ—which, Paul stated emphatically, "is better by far" (v. 23). In other words, Paul knew that as a Christian he would win no matter what happened. "I eagerly expect and hope," he wrote, "that I will in no way be ashamed, but will have sufficient courage so that now as always Christ will be exalted in my body, whether by life *or* by death" (v. 20).

Paul's eternal perspective enabled him to face these problems and troubles with great courage and comfort. In the light of eternity, he called them "momentary troubles," and "so," he said, "we fix our eyes not on what is *seen,* but on what is *unseen.* For what is seen is temporary, but what is unseen is *eternal*" (2 Cor. 4:17-18).

4. Paul was encouraged by positive feedback. As we've already noted, Paul evidently wrote a letter to the Corinthians that is not included in the biblical record (see 1 Cor. 5:9). In that letter he was quite frontal and specific regarding their failures and sins. Paul, in his humanness was fearful that the Corinthians might not only reject his exhortations but him as well. This is why at one point in his letter he became very vulnerable. "We have spoken freely to you, Corinthians, and open wide our hearts to you. We are not withholding our affection from you, but you are withholding yours from us. As a fair exchange," he wrote, "open wide your hearts also" (2 Cor. 6:11-13).

Later Paul recorded that he had received a special report from Titus that had reassured him. He told them that this report greatly *encouraged* him. "In all our troubles my joy knows no bounds" (7:4).

Paul's specific response to this positive feedback regarding their attitudes towards both him and what he had written to them earlier, speaks for itself:

> For when we came into Macedonia, this body of ours had no rest, but we were harrassed at every turn—conflicts on the outside, fears within. But God, who *comforts* the downcast, *comforted* us by the coming of Titus, and not only by his coming but also by the *comfort* you had given him. He told us about your longing for me, your deep sorrow, your ardent concern for me, so that my joy was greater than ever (vv. 5-7).

Paul's humanness is probably never clearer than in this passage. Although he was a great apostle, and one of God's choicest servants, he needed love and acceptance from those he ministered to. At times he felt rejected because of his unwillingness to compromise the truth, and it caused him great emotional pain. But when God's message was well received—as it eventually was by the Corinthians—and when he was reassured by their love and acceptance of him, he responded like any one of us would—with great joy. He was indeed encouraged!

Note, too, that part of Paul's encouragement resulted from the encouragement given to Titus by the Corinthians (v. 7). Because he was comforted, he was able to comfort Paul. The fact that Christians are God's primary means for encouraging other Christians is clearly outlined in this section of Paul's letter.

5. Paul was encouraged by the spiritual progress in the lives of those he ministered to. This, of course, is intricately related to *positive feedback.* But it deserves separate attention. Initially Paul's "painful letter" caused deep sorrow in the hearts of the Corinthians. Paul deeply regretted this for he did not wish to discourage anyone (vv. 8-9). Evidently he felt the severity of the letter may have caused more harm than good. But the positive feedback from Titus changed all that. *"Now* I am happy, not because you were made sorry, but because your sorrow led you to repentance" (v. 9). Their godly sorrow plus their affirmation of love for Paul turned Paul's sorrow into happiness. "By all this," he wrote, *"we are encouraged!"* (v. 13)

6. *Paul was encouraged by the power of God that was evident in his life when he felt weak.* Paul was one of those unique biblical personalities who was called to fulfill God's will in unusual ways. In fact, he was given revelations from God so profound that he could not express them in words (12:4). If he did choose to express them, he knew people would tend to idolize and worship him rather than the One he served. Though he must have been tempted often to share these things, especially when his apostleship was being questioned by fellow Christians, he refrained.

But God knew that Paul was human and in a moment of weakness he might take advantage of the situation and hinder his ministry by misusing this information. Consequently, Paul stated that God allowed him to have a "thorn in the flesh" to keep him "from becoming conceited because of these surpassingly great revelations" (v. 7).

We do not know what this thorn was. Some think it was a physical problem—such as blindness or even physical disfigurement. We could also speculate that it may have been some kind of psychological weakness. Nevertheless, Paul reported that he "pleaded with the Lord" on *three* different occasions that He might remove the problem. But God spoke directly to Paul and said, "No" and told him that His grace would see him through. In fact, the Lord stated to Paul that His "power is made perfect in weakness" (v. 9).

This direct knowledge of God's purpose in allowing him to have this "thorn" gave him a whole new perspective on the problems he faced. Because Paul saw *meaning* in his trials and tribulations, he was able to *accept* those difficulties as a means to a more effective ministry—even to rejoice in them. Thus he wrote, "that is *why,* for Christ's sake, I delight in weakness, in insults, in hardships, in persecutions, in difficulties. For when I am *weak,* I am strong" (v. 10).

Some Important Observations

At least two observations can be made regarding what we've learned thus far.

First, in four out of the six ways in which Paul was encouraged, God used other Christians to encourage him. The purpose he saw in his own troubles related to *those* he could help in their troubles. He also relied heavily on the *prayers* of his fellow Christians for deliverance. And *positive feedback* from those he ministered to as well as their *spiritual progress* encouraged him greatly. These human factors blended with his *eternal perspective* and God's *power* which was revealed in his own weaknesses enabled Paul to face some difficult situations with unusual joy and thanksgiving to God. This shows us that God's primary means for encouragement involves Christians helping other Christians face life's difficulties victoriously.

Second, Paul was an unusual individual in God's plan, facing extreme problems which called for unusual solutions. It is dangerous to generalize too specifically from Paul's life, for even very few New Testament Christians experienced the difficulties he faced as God's special apostle.

However, his experiences and the way he was encouraged apply to *all* Christians—no matter what our own difficulties. Few Christians living today can—or will ever—identify completely with Paul's specific experiences and the causes for his suffering. All of us at times face intense moments of physical and psychological distress. Though they may not be caused by the enemies of the Gospel, what encouraged Paul also encourages us. And this leads us to some very specific 20th-century applications.

God's Comfort Today

1. We too need to see purpose in our difficulties. It is in times of trouble that we need to remind ourselves of Roman 8:28, "that in *all things* God works for the *good* of those who love Him, who have been called according to His purpose." To experience the reality of this verse and this promise, we must look for the "good" in every situation, no matter how difficult it is.

I am reminded of Dr. Victor Frankl, who, as an educated Jew, faced the ravages of a Nazi concentration camp. Like others around him, he was horribly depressed and discouraged and in a desperate state physically because of malnutrition. He actually felt as if he would die at any moment.

As a practicing psychiatrist before being taken captive by the Nazis, he had developed an approach to counseling called logotherapy. More specifically, he tried to help his patients see *meaning* in suffering.

He even utilized the approach on himself. The *only* meaning he could see in what was happening was that someday he would live to tell others that his therapy worked—and in this way help them to experience the reality of his theory. While being held captive, he pictured himself lecturing to a group on the subject of logotherapy, telling them how he survived his horrible experiences. By seeing this *meaning* in his experience, he gained sufficient strength to live to tell the story to thousands of people. In fact, my wife and I heard him share the story one evening in a special lecture series at the University of Dallas.

If this process worked for a man who did not claim to be a Christian, how much more could it work for a believer? What meaning can *you* see in your moment of discouragement? Is God preparing you to help someone else? Is He preparing you for a greater responsibility? Will this make you a better parent, pastor, or friend? By seeing meaning in difficult situations, you can become a more mature Christian—and often rise above the negative emotions you are feeling.

One time when I was disillusioned and in emotional turmoil, I studied the lives of Christians that God has used in special ways. As I read, I noticed a pattern. I saw that God often used suffering to eventually enable them to help others who were going through the same deep waters. That sudden insight changed my psychological disposition. It enabled me to experience joy in the midst of turmoil and to make sense out of what seemed chaotic.

This should not be too surprising in view of what Paul experienced. If even non-Christians can experience a degree of relief from stress, it should not surprise us that God desires to use this process in our lives too.

2. *To experience encouragement we need the prayer support of our fellow Christians.* Prayer worked for Paul and it can work for us. It is a divine resource, but it definitely involves other

Christians. God is interested in every aspect of our lives, including physical and emotional pain. Our problem is that we don't take prayer seriously enough. Paul exhorted the Philippians:

Do not be anxious about anything, but *in everything,* by *prayer and petition,* with thanksgiving, present your requests to God. And the *peace of God,* which transcends all understanding, will guard your hearts and your minds in Christ Jesus (Phil. 4:6-7).

All of us need Christian friends we can share our deepest concerns with, knowing they will faithfully pray for us. This means developing relationships that build trust and confidence. It is true that we should draw on the prayer support of as many Christians as possible. But for this process to be effective we need a smaller group of faithful prayer partners who will pray regularly and persistently.

The opposite of course is also true. In order to *be encouragers,* we need to be faithful prayer supporters, especially for missionaries and others who live outside of our culture and face dangers we usually do not face.

The Christians in our own church were deeply moved one day by the call for prayer of one of our own missionary families at Fellowship Bible Church. Larry and Kathy Walker and their four lovely daughters were leaving us to go back to Guatemala where guerilla activity had reached their own home town. As Larry shared their need for prayer, he was obviously fearful, but he was willing to go—*if* we would pray for them. This experience probably comes closer to Paul's experience than any I've encountered for quite some time. My heart was touched.

How faithful are you in the prayer support of those who represent you on the "firing line" of Christian missions?

3. We need to develop an eternal perspective when facing earthly problems. Few of us have faced the problems Paul faced —threats on our lives, physical beatings, unprotected exposure to the elements and an actual shortage of food. But persecution and suffering are not the only problems Christians face where we need to develop an *eternal perspective.*

I have a close friend named Omar Brubaker who is about my age. For a number of years we taught together at Moody Bible

Institute in Chicago. He is one of the most devoted and sensitive Christians I know.

A couple of years ago his body was attacked by incurable leukemia. Little by little, he has been losing ground in his battle against this dreaded disease.

One day while in Chicago I called Omar to let him know I was concerned about him and praying for him and his family. He had just gone through a difficult time in the hospital. While talking with my friend, I was deeply touched by his perspective on his problem. It was definitely eternal! A few weeks later, I received this letter in the mail:

Greetings from the Word: "The Lord reigns, let the earth be glad; let the distant shores rejoice. . . . Let those who love the Lord hate evil, for He guards the lives of His faithful ones" (Ps. 97:1, 10).

It is thrilling to read the words "the Lord reigns." He is sovereign. He is in control in my life—and I am sure you can say the same for yours. I appreciate the words by John Parker in the song, *God Holds the Key:*

"God holds the key of all unknown, and I am glad . .
If other hands should hold the key, or
If He trusted it to me, I might be sad. . . .

"What if tomorrow's cares were here without its rest . . . ?
I'd rather He'd unlock the day and as the hours
Swing open say, 'Thy will is best' . . .

"The very dimness of my sight makes me secure
For groping in my misty way I feel His hand
I hear Him say, 'My help is sure.'

"I cannot read His future plans,
But this I know,
I have the smiling of His face and
All the refuge of His grace,
While here below.

"Enough; this covers all my wants, and so
I rest
For, what I cannot, He can see, and, in His
Care I safe shall be, forever blessed."

With this letter, Omar ministered to me in ways that I did not minister to him. My own commitment to Christ was deepened by that experience. Omar's eternal perspective helped me refocus my own priorities.

4. We all need "positive feedback" to be encouraged. Let no one say we don't! If Paul did, we certainly do too.

Paul let the whole world know how good it made him feel when Titus reported the affection and concern the Corinthians had for him. "My *joy*," he wrote, "was greater than ever" (2 Cor. 7:7).

Again, this principle can be reversed. If positive feedback encourages us, it also encourages others. Let us never be guilty of withholding from people that which can encourage them and help them be more effective servants of Jesus Christ.

5. To be encouraged we need to know when people we are ministering to are making spiritual progress in their lives. There is only one way for those who minister to you to know what is happening in your life. You must make it known. Then when you do it will encourage them.

One of the most encouraging letters I have received recently came from a member of our own church. With this person's permission, I share this excerpt with you, for it may encourage you as well.

> I am very much a babe in Christ, even though I have professed Him as my Lord for six years. I realize that I didn't *really* know Him—I only knew about Him and about the Word. I could quote portions of Scripture and take lessons from them somewhat and relate to the teachings and experiences of others, but I didn't have much of a relationship with Jesus, mostly because I neglected Him. . . . He has humbled me—I had false spiritual pride and sense of "wisdom" that made me virtually unteachable. . . . He has changed my heart and I would be a

willing sponge to soak up all that is made available to me. . . .

I am very grateful for His grace and faithfulness—in spite of myself, He has patiently nudged me in the direction of some beautiful people who have helped me along the way and finally to Fellowship Bible Church. I wish I could better express the excitement I feel and the joy in my spirit!

This letter represents positive feedback, not only to those who teach the Word from the platform, but to the whole body of Christ. We all need this kind of positive feedback for it enables us to keep on ministering to people in a faithful way.

6. *We need to realize that God's power can be released in our lives during periods of weakness.* The reason for this is quite clear. We rely less on ourselves and our own abilities and trust God more. I can't explain this phenomenon completely, but I know it is true.

This does not mean we cannot be used of the Lord when we feel strong, but our confidence should be in Christ. This is why Paul wrote to the Ephesians, "Be strong in the Lord and in His mighty power" (Eph. 6:10).

Times of weakness also drive us to our knees for divine guidance and help. If we're honest, most of us will admit that some of our most meaningful times of prayer are when we have no choice . . . when our human alternatives are gone. We *must* depend on God in those moments. In those instances, God's power is released in our lives as never before.

I do not pray for these periods to come into my life. But when they come, I pray more and am more motivated to place my confidence in Jesus Christ.

Life Response

Following are six brief prayers that capture the practical lessons we can learn from Paul regarding mutual encouragement:

> Lord, help me to see *purpose* and meaning in those times of discouragement and difficulty that come into my life—especially that I might be able to identify with others and help them in their times of trial.

Lord, help me to seek the *prayer support* of fellow Christians during times of distress and discomfort. Help me to faithfully pray for others who have similar needs.

Lord, help me to develop an *eternal perspective* on my earthly problems—to see that life on this earth is really very short compared to eternity and what awaits me there as one of Your children.

Lord, help me to hear *positive feedback* from my Christian brothers and sisters when I am discouraged. Help me to give *positive feedback* to those who also need encouragement.

Lord, help me to experience the encouragement that comes from helping someone experience spiritual progress. Remind me to encourage others by giving positive feedback to those who've helped me grow spiritually.

Lord, help me to thank You and to even delight in times of weakness and difficulty, for Your Word teaches me that "when I am weak, then I am strong." This is a difficult prayer, Lord, but Paul did it and I pray that I can too.

If you enjoyed this study, you'll want to read two other Victor books by Dr. Getz.

Building Up One Another

discusses 12 specific "one another" commands of the New Testament and shows how every believer is to take part in building up others.

Loving One Another

focuses on evangelism that begins in love. It tells you how to find greater unity and fruitfulness, in your life and in your church.